Girls' Life

Head-to-Toe Guide to YOU

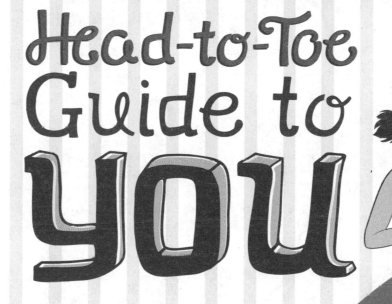

From the creators of
Girls' Life magazine

Edited by Sarah Wassner Flynn

Scholastic Inc.

New York   Toronto   London   Auckland   Sydney
Mexico City   New Delhi   Hong Kong

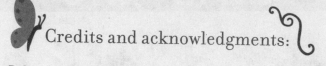

Credits and acknowledgments:

Here's to Karen Bokram and her amazing team of *Girls' Life* writers and editors for their contributions to this book, including Katie Abbondanza, Sandy Fertman Ryan, Amanda Forr, Kristen Kemp, Patricia McNamara, Lisa Mulcahy, and Michelle Silver

page 32 - glass of water © Ncbojsak | Dreamstime.com
page 52 - bathtub - © Wichittra Srisunon | Dreamstime.com
page 68 - tooth - © ceneri/istockphoto.com
page 105 - present - © gollykim/istockphoto.com
page 120 - bananas - © jut13/istockphoto.com

ISBN 978-0-545-20236-7

Published by Scholastic Inc.
SCHOLASTIC and associated logos are trademarks and/or registered trademarks of Scholastic Inc.

12 11 10 9 8 7 6   12 13 14/0

illustrated by Bill Thomas and Dynamo Limited
Designed by Sara Gillingham and Angela Jun
Hand-lettering and cover design by Angela Navarra
Printed in the U.S.A.   40
First printing, April 2010

This book is for informational purposes only and not intended as medical advice and should not replace the advice of or treatment by any health-care professional. You should consult your doctor with questions about your physical and mental well-being. This book should be considered a supplemental resource only.

contents

Introduction

One morning you wake up and you feel a little different, you look in the mirror and you look a little different, too. You might be thinking, "Whose body is this?" Up until now, growing up has been a gradual thing. But in the early teen years, all sorts of new stuff starts to happen, like the appearance of breasts, body hair, and the dreaded zits. Some of it can bring a welcome change, but puberty can also be a little strange and confusing.

Here's the good news: You're definitely not alone as you adjust to these changes. But we know it may not always feel that way, especially when it seems like all the girls in your class have perfect skin, hair, and bodies—and you're feeling anything but flawless.

All of these changes are probably making you anything but BFFs with your body. Or even frenemies. But we have a secret to let you in on: You're beautiful. No really, you are. And to help you realize this fact, we've put together this guide to give you the straight scoop on all that's going on in your body. From skin issues to self-esteem, we've got you covered from head to toe.

Dear Readers,

With only five days to go until eighth-grade spring break, I was happily packing for a ski trip with my dad and stepmother. Then my mom got a phone call. **Change of plans.** My father had decided that the closest I was going to get to powder was the sugar on top of my morning pancakes. Being sent unpacking would have been fine save one small detail—**my mother** had been planning a trip to Greece and was not in any position to cancel it. So my father—with visions of Vail dancing in his head—and my mother—unwavering in her pursuit of baklava—came up with a compromise. **I'd spend** the week visiting my seventy-year-old great-aunt Connie at her retirement condo in Florida. *Oh, joy.*

To my mother's credit, **she painted** the most tropical picture she could. I had never been to visit my great-aunt, and I bought into the whole sand/surf/sun-and-**fun story**. As quickly as I had dug out my earmuffs, I was now buying a new bikini. **Maybe this won't be so bad**, I told myself.

By the time Aunt Connie picked me up from the airport, I **started** to get a sinking feeling in my stomach about this whole week. But I gamely smiled and said how great it was to be in Sarasota and how much I was looking forward to **hanging out** with her. After getting to the condo, it didn't take me long to uncover that my aunt lived in a "senior community" and the only way I'd see another teen that week was if I turned on the TV. I thought I was going to throw up. And then I did.

After sitting on the throne with my head in my hands, praying some coma would overtake me, I looked down to realize that the sinking feeling I'd had in the airport wasn't clairvoyance—it was cramps. I had just gotten my period for the very *first time*.

I'd love to say I mustered the guts to tell Aunt Connie, that we had a moment of intergenerational bonding that kicked off a wonderful week of swapping life stories. But the truth is I first had a good cry, realizing that my best friend was nine hundred miles away and my mother was probably on her third serving of souvlaki. Then **I madly began digging** through cabinets looking for anything slightly resembling a pad or tampon. No dice.

I can't tell you how much fun it was to hang out in ninety degree heat by the pool while I sat in my shorts, *praying the Kleenex* wouldn't fall out of my undies.

Thankfully, for whatever lack of timing my body graced me with, my mother didn't lack in the information department. I may have been ill-prepared with supplies (if this story doesn't scream cautionary tale, I don't know what does), but I was well-armed with info about **my changing body**. I knew getting my period was an important and great thing. It meant I was joining a sisterhood of women all over the world, experiencing something unique and magical about *being a girl*. I was now bonded to my mother, my grandmother, and even my great-aunt Connie. If I only had a book to help me through that time in Florida. Luckily you do.

♡ KB

body basics

Everyone goes through puberty at some point—that's just life for ya. Of course, figuring out exactly when and how long you'll be going through it, well, that's a mystery, since everyone is different. Still, studies say that most girls begin puberty around age eleven and it lasts about five to six years from start to finish. Take comfort in knowing that it will be over one day—and you're not the only girl to grow three inches during the summer or to sprout underarm hair practically overnight.

But before we get too ahead of ourselves, let's start with the basics. Puberty, as your health-class teacher would define it, is the transition you go through when your body secretes new hormones and makes some changes. In other words, you start looking more, well, womanly, and start feeling weird and wonderful, all at the same time.

the growth spurt

Nope, it's not your imagination. Your bones are growing super-fast. Get this—during the total span of adolescence, the average person grows a full foot. Weight typically increases twenty to thirty pounds, about ten pounds a year. In a world where models look too frail to stand up straight, it's not surprising girls often freak at putting on so much weight so quickly. Gaining inches and pounds is not only normal, it's supposed to happen. The last thing you want to do is try to stop it.

Besides going up a dress size, your fave jeans may suddenly become Capri pants. And it may seem odd to peer down at the top of your mom's head as she yells at you for not emptying the dishwasher. Your legs may even ache as your bones and muscles stretch.

Trust us—most of you will not keep growing until you're seeing eye-to-eye with an NBA player. *Your growth spurt will sputter out,* most likely around the time you get your period. If boys taunt you about your height, it's because they would kill to be in your shoes instead of feeling like a shorty in their own. For now, you may be gazing down at your crush's head instead of into his eyes when slow dancing, but he should sprout about two years after you do.

Lots of girls spend lots of time wishing. Taller girls wish to lose inches (so not gonna happen). Shorter girls just want a bit more height (may happen, may not). Regardless, make the most of what you have and be proud of it. Wear flats if you want to, but don't think you need to avoid

is it *puberty?*

TYPICAL SIGNS THAT YOUR BODY'S BEGINNING TO CHANGE

* A sudden growth spurt
* Weight gain, especially in the hips, chest, and thighs
* Body odor, oily hair, and skin breakouts
* Hair growth in the underarm area, on the legs, and in the pubic area
* Vaginal discharge and your first period
* Moodiness, including stints of sadness and anger
* A stronger interest in boys

tot! Shorter girls tell us it's easier to be taken seriously when you use a strong voice and project confidence (no shuffling down the hall and speaking to your shoes). Try to steer clear of pigtails and cutesy clothes—those styles can just make you look younger.

chunky heels or boots. Walk with your chin up and shoulders back.

Then there are girls who have the opposite problem. We're talking to you, small stuff. Nothing like having the whole sophomore class patting you on the head—hello, you're not a

And remember, there's no height requirement for being taken seriously. Showcase your brains, talent, and abilities, and people will take note, no matter where you are on the height chart.

help! i'm a late bloomer!

Although studies say most girls' bodies start to change around age eleven, each of us follow our own schedule. Some girls get breasts as early as age seven, while others don't develop until they're seventeen (or even older!). Still, it can be pretty frustrating when you're the only one of your friends who doesn't need a bra—or you've been about a foot shorter than everyone else for what seems like decades. But rest assured that your time to grow (in one way or another) is coming soon. For the most part, puberty is based on genetics, so ask your mom or an older sister about their experiences. If you're really worried, have your parents take you to your doctor—he or she will run a few tests to make sure everything's OK.

what's happening to my chest?

up may be event-worthy, **you might need to remind relatives that your body is a private matter**—and updates about it don't belong on the family blog. One embarrassed girl tells us, *"My mom thinks it's perfectly OK to share my bra size with anyone. She even wrote about it in our Christmas letter!"*

All of the sudden, your once-flat chest is filling out and breasts are starting to appear. *Not to worry, we're all in the same boat.* Ultimately, small- and large-chested gals have a lot of the same worries: **Do my clothes look OK? Are people staring at my chest? Why do my friends all have bigger (or smaller) boobs than me? Are my breasts done growing?**

It can be a difficult experience when something so obvious to the world is happening (or not happening, as the case may be) to your body. While seeing their *"little girl"* growing

If an **adult** makes comments, tell the person it makes you uncomfortable and to please stop. While puberty happens to everyone and is certainly not anything shameful, *it is also your personal business.*

Despite the fact that getting breasts is inevitable, many girls worry that they aren't developing as quickly as they should. The thing is, your body is on a timetable that is unique to you. **Some girls bust out at an early age;** others will remain small-chested. Some girls will get more than they expected, and others will look at their moms and wonder if the breast gene skipped a generation.

Whatever size you have, you're absolutely normal. There's no such thing as a right size. And for the record, if one breast is larger than the other, join the club. Almost all women have one breast slightly bigger, and while you're still growing they each develop at different rates. So hang in there—it should all even out in the end.

hello, hips!

Right around the same time you fill out on top, you'll probably also get a little extra on the sides. Again, every girl's body develops at its own pace. Still, it's surprising when you first notice them. *"I used to buy clothes in the children's department,"* says Mindy, fourteen, **"but then I got hips, and suddenly, I had to move to juniors."**

One reader who hated her new hips at first, woke up one day and realized she likes the way they look: *"Jeans look better on me with curves. I just had to get used to them,"* she says. You too will get used to them, and once you do, you will probably discover that, hey, **having curves is cool.**

you may break out . . . don't freak out

For years, you rolled out of bed and out of the house without thinking twice about your face. Now, you take one peek at the mirror and gasp in horror at the state of your skin. What used to be smooth as a baby's you-know-what is now riddled with red marks. **Zits. One of the worst aspects of puberty.**

Unfortunately, acne and oily skin are pretty much unavoidable at this time. Your glands are going wild, thanks to all of the hormones running through your body. Throw in some bacteria and perspiration and voilà—**a breakout is born.**

We've got plenty more on keeping your skin clear in **Chapter 4,** but what we can't stress enough is the importance of keeping your face clean. That means washing twice a day with an anti-acne product, don't pick, and treat spots with benzoyl peroxide. If things get really out of control, ask Mom or Dad to take you to a dermatologist. Plenty of excellent acne treatments are available by prescription.

No matter what you do, remind yourself that you're just one in about twenty million teens who **battle blemishes on a daily basis.** Besides, even the girl with the most gorgeous skin ever gets a zit (or two—or twenty!) every once in a while.

swinging moods

Up to this point, we've addressed the bodily changes of puberty. But something is going on beyond the physical. We're referring to mood swings. It's not uncommon to throw your arms around Mom and give her a smooch on the cheek one minute, and the next, **barricade yourself** in your room 'cause you can't take her nagging for one more second.

Or maybe you think you have the best buds in the world. Moments later, one says something that rubs you the wrong way, and you're convinced that the whole bunch is out to get you. **Your brain—in addition to your body—is trying to get used to those hormones.** You're not going crazy, and this will end once your body and mind have a chance to adapt to the new hormone levels.

In the meantime? Think privacy. If you're out of control, let everyone know you need some alone time. It also helps to write your changing feelings in a journal. It's a great way to get emotions off your, um, chest. And talk with buds—they're going through this experience, too.

Relax and try not to take everything too seriously. We know this is easier said than done when you're feeling hypersensitive. Yet, it's still good, solid advice.

one more thing . . .

Phew—lots going on, right? Between your body, your moods, and everything else, it's no wonder you're feeling so overwhelmed. Watching yourself morph before your very eyes— and everybody else's—is no piece of cake. You can feel like you've lost control of your body, but things will slow down soon. And just remember, no matter what's occurring in your body, you do have control over the important things, like being yourself— breasts, hips, zits, and all.

everything about periods, period

plus other down-there details

2

Your first-ever period is a surefire sign that yes, puberty has one hundred percent arrived. Once you get your period, you'll be dealing with it every twenty-eight-or-so days for the next, oh, forty years or so.

Some of you may be excited by that tidbit—you're so ready to catch up to friends and feel grown up. For others, "that time of the month" signifies something scary—cramps, zit cream, even fears about leaving childhood behind. If you fall into the latter category, don't stress: You have every right to be freaked out about your period. It's a completely new situation, and it can be downright nerve-wracking to even think about, let alone discuss with someone else.

The Facts: Periods

But truth be told, getting your period is really not that scary of a sitch. It's a pretty simple thing, actually. **What happens is this:** Each month, an egg from your ovary takes a little trip over to your uterus, which builds up with tissue and blood while awaiting the egg's arrival. When your egg isn't fertilized along the way, all that extra tissue and blood (and the egg) make an exit through your vaginal opening. That's your period.

And not only is your period a symbol of your leap into womanhood, but it's also a sign that you're **healthy.** A regular period means all systems are go in your body. You are producing the right amount of hormones that are needed not only to send messages from your brain to your ovaries (to release the unfertilized egg), but also to protect your bones, brain, and other parts of your body.

Now that you've got those bases covered, on to the, oh, probably **zillion-and-one** questions you have about your period.

Q: "When will I get my period? I need to know!"

A: Most girls get their first period around eleven or twelve. However, some girls get their periods as early as nine, and some as late as sixteen. Every girl is different. But we can pretty much assure you that, sooner or later, you're gonna get it.

Q: "What does it feel like to have your period? Does it hurt?"

A: As most girls who have their periods will tell you, it doesn't really feel like anything at all. In fact, many girls feel absolutely nothing. Still, there are some side effects girls feel just before or during their periods—abdominal cramps, sore breasts, bloating, lower back pain, headaches, zit outbreaks, and low energy. You can talk to your mom or doctor about the possibility of taking medication.

But before you resign yourself to a monthly ugh-fest, there are some things you can do (phew). To start, ask yourself this one question: Got milk? Researchers at St. Luke's-Roosevelt Hospital in New York found that 1,200 mg of calcium daily—either through sources like fortified orange juice, yogurt, milk, or through supplements—can decrease period symptoms by approximately fifty percent.

Or try aromatherapy. Combine thirteen drops clary sage oil plus two drops of ylang-ylang oil with fifteen drops vitamin E oil (all available at health food stores), and massage the mixture on the cramping area. For low energy, a handful of raisins (high in iron) often does the trick.

17

As for the breakouts? It's best to avoid acne cleansers and medicated pads if your skin behaves normally the rest of the month. Just dab some drying lotion on the spot, and try not to pick. (See Chapter 4 for more tips on fighting zits.) It won't take long (really!) before you're able to pick up all the unique things your period brings about in your body tricks of your own to deal with them.

Q: "How long will it last?"

A: Your period could last up to eight days, or it may only last two. Be prepared, say most girls, for it to flow about three to six days. And keep in mind that your periods can change every month—you might have it for two days during one month, and then five days the next. That's totally normal.

Q: "Will I get really cranky, like my older sister does? She blames everything on PMS!"

A: Some girls have definite mood swings because of surging hormones. A few days before getting their periods, many say they start to feel some effects of PMS (premenstrual syndrome, which, yes, affects girls and is very real). Some feel cranky or irritable. Others get a little blue and weepy. The good news is that the swings are temporary and pretty tolerable (check out the "Beat the Blues" sidebar on page 24). If you feel severe mood swings or experience extremely painful cramps, though, you should see a doctor.

Q: "Once I get it, how will I know when it's coming next?"

A: For the most part, girls get their periods every twenty-eight days or so. While some can predict the exact day of their next period, other girls have irregular cycles and may be off by a week or more. You may be even more irregular when you first start getting your period, skipping a whole month or two. This is perfectly normal—nothing to panic over. Says Jerry, twelve, **"When you first start getting it, you can never predict when it might strike. I once got mine twice in one month."** Regardless, keep track of your flow in a calendar or planner. Over time, it will be easier to tell what time of the month you can expect **"that time of the month."**

> Q: "I'm terrified I will be caught totally off guard. What can I do?"

A: This is an extreme fear for girls. Says Kristi, ten, *"I always hear about girls going to dances in white dresses and walking out with a big red spot!"* First of all, of the millions of letters we've received about periods over the years, only a handful of girls said they were busted in a public place with a surprise stain. But, OK, there's certainly a fair chance you'll be surprised at least one time. If you're at school, every nurse has a supply of pads in her office for this situation. You should also

Ultra Thin

Super-Absorbent

Tampon

keep emergency supplies in your locker, and a sweater you can wrap around your waist just in case. Or, just ask a fellow female for a pad (no biggie). If that's a bust, fold a thick layer of toilet paper to form a pad, and place it in your underpants. Be sure to wrap it around the crotch of the underwear to keep it in place.

19

Q: "What if it's too late and people can see a stain?"

A: You can call a parent for a change of clothes, ask to borrow something out of the lost and found, or even change into your gym or practice stuff a little early. It's also helpful to know that no one ever actually died of embarrassment. (Really.)

Q: "Which is better— pads or tampons?"

A: There's no better or worse, just what's more comfortable for you. A lot of girls are nervous about using tampons at first, so they stick with pads. *"I sleep with thick pads, but use thin pads when I go to school so they're not bulky,"* says Tara,

betcha didn't know this...

And you thought you'd heard it all. We went in pursuit of some trivia facts about your period.

☀ The first tampon with applicator was sold in the United States in **1936**.

☀ A hundred years ago, the average age for getting your period was **14.8** years old. Now, it's twelve!

☀ The average number of periods you'll have in a lifetime is **480**.

fifteen. Some girls choose to never use tampons at all, which is perfectly fine. Other girls, who swear by tampons, say they are "*comfortable, more reliable, and you hardly know they're there.*" Suggests Kasey, fifteen, "If you're going to use tampons for the first time, you may want to put a mirror on the floor so you can see exactly what you're doing." Just be sure to change your tampon every four to six hours. For info on how to insert a tampon, check the instructions in any box of tampons.

Q: "Which brands work best?"

A: There are choices out there. Some *GL* readers recommend pads with wings for less chance of staining (the product wraps around the edges of your underwear). As for tampons, you can choose between slender, regular, super, and super-plus sizes, depending on the heaviness of your flow. Several girls say ultra-glide is easiest to use.

Q: "Should I tell anyone I got it?"

A: *Absolutely,* but it's your choice who and how to tell. In a recent survey of *GL* readers, most told their mothers. "**Your mom will be a lot cooler than you think,**" says one reader. "*If you're calm, she will be, too.*" The majority of girls say they also told their best friends, whether the friends had gotten their periods already or not. "**It's not something to be embarrassed about,**" says Beth, eleven. In fact, L.D., eleven, sums it up like this, "*When you do get it, congratulations! You're a woman!*"

Q: "If I am protected with a pad or tampon, will anyone be able to tell I have my period?"

Q: "I hear I can catch a period if my friend is having hers. Is that true?"

A: No, the only way anyone will ever suspect you have your period is if you tell them outright—or scream down the hallway, *"Guess what I just got?!"*

A: No, getting your period is not contagious. However, when friends (who already got their periods) hang out a lot, **they sometimes end up on the same cycle.** This also happens a lot with moms and daughters, since they live together.

Q. "What if I go to buy pads or tampons, and the check-out guy is from my class?"

A: Of course, if you have a choice of stores, you can shop elsewhere. If that's not an option, ask your mom or older sister if she'll pick up the supplies. Or, decide to not be embarrassed. After all, most of the teenage and adult women in town buy these products, so chances are the boy deals with this all the time. If he's cool, he won't say a thing. If he's a jerk about it, who cares what he thinks?

Q: "Do I have to go to the doctor when I get my period?"

A: Once you get your period, you should probably ask your parents to take you to a *gynecologist*, a doctor who specializes in female reproductive health. Why? Well, the American College of Obstetricians and Gynecologists recommends a visit to the gynecologist when you're between the ages of thirteen and fifteen—so that's probably right around the time you'll get your first period.

Seeing a gynecologist doesn't necessarily mean you need to undergo an internal pelvic exam. Instead, you can ask your new doctor all of your health-related questions. Some girls just aren't comfortable discussing certain topics with Mom. While it's important to find a trusted adult in your world to talk to, your doctor (who literally talks about this kind of stuff all day, every day) is a valuable resource. You're free to ask your doctor any question you want, **no matter how awkward or weird you think it is,** and your conversation will be private and confidential. And, remember, if you're having problems with missed or skipped periods, bad cramping, or heavy or prolonged bleeding, you definitely need to see a doctor, whether it be your family practitioner or a gynecologist.

23

SUGGESTIONS FOR CHASING AWAY PMS

- ☀ Put a heating pad on your belly, read a book, and drink warm milk, tea, or hot chocolate

- ☀ Use your journal to express yourself when you're feeling grumpy or crampy

- ☀ Take a long bath with relaxing essential oils, such as lavender

- ☀ Hang with a pet

- ☀ Three words: chocolate-covered pretzels

- ☀ Go for a brisk walk or a bike ride. Exercise is proven to ease PMS symptoms, we swear

- ☀ Drink raspberry tea—it'll mellow your cramps

- ☀ Deep breathe. As you inhale, picture breathing in happiness. As you exhale, picture releasing tension

- ☀ Remind yourself that you're not going crazy, and that this will be over soon

test your *period smarts!*

TRUE OR FALSE

THINK YOU'RE THE PERIOD KNOW-IT-ALL?
PUT YOURSELF TO THE TEST!

1. You can lose a tampon inside of you, if you don't put it in right.

2. When you menstruate, you normally lose about a pint of blood.

3. When girls in the same age group have been living together for a while, like in a camp bunk, they tend to get their periods at the same time.

4. Periods normally last a week.

5. PMS is all in your mind.

1. False. There is limited space inside your vagina—with only one way out!

2. False. On average, a girl loses about three tablespoons of blood each month.

3. Weird, but true. Girls living around each other for a while tend to get "in sync" with one another's cycles.

4. False. The average period lasts only four or five days, but it can really vary since every body is different.

5. False. PMS affects your emotions, but it is the result of physical changes.

the down-low on "down there"

By now, you should be all set on period facts. But there's a whole lot of other stuff going on in and around your vagina during other parts of the month. As you're probably well aware, your vagina doesn't just dry up like the Sahara once your period is over. Rather, you'll experience discharge throughout the month—that whitish, clear, sticky stuff you notice in your undies. This is just part of being a girl. And discharge is actually good for you because it's the vagina's way of cleaning itself.

And if you haven't gotten your period yet? You'll probably still start to feel a little dampness down there. That's because six months to a year before their first period, girls start to produce vaginal discharge. This is how your body clears dead cells from the vagina to keep you free of infection. The fluid is usually thin and slightly sticky, but can be thick and gooey. Color ranges from clear to off-white, but if the odor is all of a sudden really bad, a color other than clear, white, or off-white, or it's accompanied by itchiness or burning, it could be a vaginal infection and you should see a doctor right away.

don't be embarrassed by odor

Just a reminder that it's one hundred percent normal for discharge to have a slight smell. All girls have some sort of smell down below, but it's not a bad odor. So breathe easy—the smell isn't strong enough to be detected by anyone.

Still, you can offset any odor by always wearing cotton underwear and breathable clothes and **showering regularly.** And whatever you do, don't buy into any of those products that promise to keep you smelling like a spring meadow, such as douches or hygiene sprays and creams. All you need to do to stay clean and healthy is to wash yourself on the outside only with a gentle soap and water when you shower.

"All my friends wear thongs, but my mom refuses to let me wear one, even under my Spandex shorts for volleyball. She says it's bad hygiene—is she right?"

After some back and forth on the issue, experts now say women who wear thongs are just as healthy down there as those with full-cut granny panties. **What can cause an infection? Wearing damp, too-tight clothing for too long. So tell your mom it's not the kind of undies you slip on—it's about staying dry.**

THE *OUTER PART* OF YOUR VAGINA IS CALLED THE "VULVA." IT IS MADE UP OF THE FOLLOWING PARTS:

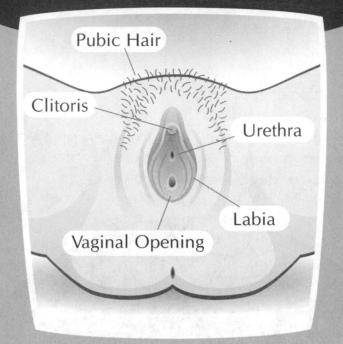

Pubic Hair

Clitoris

Urethra

Vaginal Opening

Labia

PUBIC HAIR: The triangular patch of curly hair that appears around your vagina during puberty. It protects the vagina from infection by blocking bacteria.

CLITORIS: A super sensitive bundle of nerve endings sitting just above the opening of the vagina.

URETHRA: The tube that carries pee from your bladder to the outside of your body.

VAGINAL OPENING: The largest opening between your legs. This is where a tampon is inserted during menstruation.

LABIA: The fleshy folds of skin around your vagina (also known as the "lips"). They protect the vagina from harmful bacteria.

NOT TO BE FORGOTTEN, THE *INTERIOR OF YOUR VAGINA* CONTAINS THESE IMPORTANT REPRODUCTIVE ORGANS:

OVARIES: Your two ovaries produce and store the hundreds of thousands of eggs you're born with. The number reduces to about 34,000 by puberty. Between ages twelve and seventeen, your hormones start to send signals to the ovaries to release one egg, which then travels to the uterus, ultimately becoming your period.

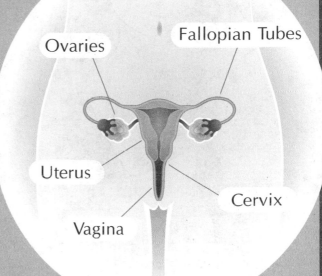

Ovaries

Fallopian Tubes

Uterus

Cervix

Vagina

UTERUS: This pear-shaped organ is the eventual home of a baby during pregnancy (the "womb"). Until then, it's where an unfertilized egg combines with blood and tissue to form the menstrual flow (your period).

FALLOPIAN TUBES: The fallopian tubes connect the ovaries to the uterus. It's where an egg passes through each month before your period.

CERVIX: The cervix connects the uterus to the vagina and lets menstrual blood out of your body.

VAGINA: A three-to-five inch canal that travels from your uterus to the outside of your body. Menstrual blood, vaginal fluids, and babies leave your body via the vagina.

Weird, but true: Thanks to its self-cleaning feature, the vagina is actually one of **the most spick-and-span areas** in your entire body. Still, because of everything that passes through it, the vagina can also be a breeding ground for bacteria. And as you know, bacteria can lead to infections, which can lead to odors, pain, itchiness, and worse if left untreated. So, to make sure you're at your healthiest, here's how to avoid the most common infections facing teen girls.

YEAST INFECTION

Nope, these don't have anything to do with eating too much bread. A yeast infection—which about seventy-five percent of women will get in their lifetime—occurs when microorganisms that naturally live in your vagina overgrow and irritate your skin. You won't have any unusual odors with a yeast infection, but you will be itchy and may see some redness around your vagina. Yeast infections may also be accompanied by a thick, white discharge (similar to cottage cheese). Even though there are over-the-counter remedies, see a doc for a diagnosis if you think you have one. **Self-diagnosis is sooo not a good idea**—often girls end up treating themselves for an infection they don't even have.

❋ Avoid It ❋

You can't always escape a yeast infection (especially if you're taking antibiotics for an illness or acne—they destroy the good bacteria that keeps yeast from overgrowing). But wearing cotton undies and looser-fitting pants, taking off your wet bathing suit soon after swimming, and eating yogurt will help you keep yeast in check.

⊙ BACTERIAL VAGINOSIS (BV)

BV is also caused by an overgrowth of bacteria that are normally found in the vagina. Warning signs include a gray or yellowish discharge, itching, pain, a burning sensation when you pee, and a fishy odor.

❋ Avoid It ❋

BV may be caused by factors like stress and fatigue, so take care of yourself! **(See Chapter 7 for tips.)** And whatever you do, don't douche (rinsing the inside of the vagina)—that'll just stir up even more bacteria.

⊙ URINARY TRACT INFECTION (UTI)

This is often caused by bacteria from the anus that travel to your urethra, and can bring on burning or pain when you pee; a frequent need to pee; strong-smelling urine; and sometimes back pain associated with a fever.

❀ Avoid It ❀

Always wipe from front to back after you pee, and hit the restroom as soon as you get the urge. Drinking lots of water and cranberry juice can also keep you UTI-free.

Avoid It

It's a good idea to use tampons during the day and change them frequently, then use a pad at night (you can keep a tampon in overnight as long as it isn't for more than eight hours).

⊚ TOXIC SHOCK SYNDROME (TSS)

Take a look at any box of tampons, and it'll warn you about the dangers of Toxic Shock Syndrome (TSS), a very, very rare but potentially fatal disease you can get if you don't change your tampons often enough or if you use them when your flow is extremely light.

one more thing . . .

We don't call 'em your private parts for no reason: Many women clam up when it comes to voicing any vagina-related issues. That's just the way our world can be sometimes. But that doesn't mean *you* should be ashamed or afraid to bring up any questions or concerns to your friends, older sisters, your mom, or your doctor. Especially if you think something might be amiss or just not right. Remember, **your vagina is a very important part of your body, just like your limbs or your brain.** And you wouldn't be embarrassed to talk about your arm, would ya?

what's your vagina iq?

TAKE THIS QUIZ TO FIND OUT!

1 How many openings does your vagina have?

A. One
B. Six
C. Two

2 What healthy snack can help you fight off yeast infections?

A. Carrots
B. Yogurt
C. Whole wheat crackers

3 What's the main function of your vaginal lips (labia)?

A. They keep out dirt and bacteria
B. They give your vagina a chance to "talk"
C. They serve no purpose

4 What kind of discharge is considered "normal"?

A. Clear or white
B. Fluid, stringy, or clumpy
C. All of the above

5 From which part of the vagina does pee exit your body?

A. The vaginal opening
B. The bladder
C. The urethra

1. C. Your vagina has two openings: the urethra and vaginal opening.

2. B. Yogurt contains probiotics, a good type of bacteria, which can fight infections.

3. A. The labia (consisting of a layer of fat, skin, and hair), serve as a barrier to bacteria and dirt.

4. C. Normal discharge varies in both color and consistency. The only cause for alarm would be if your discharge is grayish or green, is foul-smelling, has the consistency of cottage cheese, or is accompanied by itching.

5. C. Your urethra is the tube that carries urine from your bladder out of your body.

33

the ABC's (and D's) of your breasts

If we had a dollar for every girl who told us she wished her boobs were bigger/smaller/perkier/rounder/etc., we'd be rich. **Really** rich. One of puberty's many little ironies is that we all spend years dreaming of finally filling out a bikini, and then when we can, we become super self-conscious. Bottom line? Breasts can make you downright batty at this stage of your life.

Most girls develop between the ages of nine and fourteen, but if you're on the earlier or later side of this spectrum, don't stress. There's no one magical age for girls to get breasts.

Breast Basics

Believe it or not, *your breasts serve a much greater purpose than just helping you fill out that bikini.* The biological reason they're developing now is so that you can one day feed a baby—as your breasts grow, so do milk ducts beneath the surface of your skin, which will eventually allow you to produce milk. (Don't worry, there's no need to stress about making milk now. Your body knows to only do so after you give birth—**it's smart like that!**)

Think your chest might be starting to grow? There's an easy way to figure that out for sure. That's because breasts go through about five stages of development during *puberty.*

35

Some girls skip steps, while others linger at each stage for years. Here's the typical timeline for breast development, but as you read, please keep in mind this very important detail: Like all aspects of puberty, **development depends on the individual,** so do not—we repeat do not—compare your body's growth to anyone else's.

five stages of breast development

Your breasts have yet to *start growing.* They are still flat, and your nipples are raised.

Puberty starts to kick in. You'll notice a little round lump under each nipple—that's a breast bud, which contains fat tissue and milk glands. Your nipple and the areola (the skin surrounding the nipple) will get bigger and possibly darker. The area may also be a bit *tender to the touch*

or ache a bit, especially if you sleep on your stomach or wear tight clothes.

Your breasts become larger as fat deposits start to fill out the area around the nipple and areola. It's probably a good time to start *shopping for a bra.*

The areola and nipple become raised **and form a second mound above the rest of the breasts,** which continue to fill out and grow larger. (If you didn't get your period during stage 3, you probably will now.)

Hello, breasts! By this stage, your chest has likely reached its final destination, although certain life changes like pregnancy and weight gain or loss can once again **alter their size and shape.**

shapes and sizes

There's no normal shape, size, or color for your breasts, nipples, or areola. Breasts can be small or large, and point up or down. Nipples can stick out or in, and can be pale pink to dark brown. And the size of your nipples and areola could be small or large, too.

Chests not only vary from woman to woman, but from breast to breast, too. In fact, about half of all women have differences in breast size—and *it's usually the left breast that's larger* (weird, but true!). And if you're still growing, the smaller breast can catch up by the time you're eighteen. Plus, **breast asymmetry is quite normal** and poses no health problems—so that's one less thing to worry about.

And speaking of worrying, we bet you're doing a ton of it as you size up your breasts as compared to your friends or the girls changing next to you in gym class. We already warned you about the dangers of comparing yourself to others, but let us reiterate: **Being bigger or smaller than the other girls is so not a situation to stress over.** Just like some girls are taller, everyone develops differently. What you have now won't necessarily be forever, or maybe it is pretty darn close. Regardless, **appreciate how great your new body looks** and make the most of what you have.

Hair? Veins? Changes are happening to your breasts. Most likely, you've got nothing to worry about. Here's a roundup of the most random—but totally normal—things you might encounter . . .

hair here and there Hair near your breasts are just reactions to the hormones that are surging through the body. Just note that any random hair should be very fine, even if it is a little darker than before. If you have an excess number of hairs, show your doctor. You could have a hormonal imbalance that's treatable with medication. But a little bit of fuzz is normal—and some girls get more than others due to genetics.

stretch marks If your body fills out really quickly, sometimes your skin can't renew itself fast enough to keep up. So the dermis, the thicker, deeper layer of skin, thins in the spots where it's stretched out—like on your breasts, hips, and behind. At first, the new streaks look red. With time, they naturally fade and turn a translucent whitish color.

lumps Your breasts are full of lumps and bumps that are perfectly normal—particularly when you're developing. You can especially feel them if you're thin or small-chested. If both breasts feel the same, there is probably nothing wrong. If you feel a lump that is new or unusual and does not go away after your next period, then see your doctor. From the time a girl begins to menstruate, her breasts undergo regular changes each month. Extra fluid can collect around the breasts during your period, making them feel bumpy. These changes and lumps are usually harmless. Although it is extremely unlikely that someone your age would get breast cancer, lumps and other changes in your breasts should be checked by a doctor just to be sure.

● ● ● ● ● ● ● ● ● ●

veins If you see blue veins on your breasts, put your mind at ease. These are just normal veins that are very close to the surface of the skin and therefore are more easily seen. If your breasts have grown a lot in size recently, this might make the veins more obvious.

● ● ● ● ● ● ● ● ● ●

bumps If you see or feel a small, red bump near your nipple, it's likely a Montgomery gland. All women have them on the areola, the area around the nipples, but they're not always noticeable. The glands, which look like goose bumps, lubricate and condition. If the bump is sore or is there for more than a month, see a gynecologist.

the good, the bra & the ugly

GIRLS "BARE THEIR SOULS" ON THEIR INTRODUCTIONS TO BRA SHOPPING

"The bra department was next to the children's section. So kids were passing by, seeing me carrying five bras and my mom *talking really loudly*. One kid asked us what we were doing. I wanted to die!"

"My mom went up to the saleswoman and started telling her I was growing up now and I needed a bra—*like I wasn't even there.* Of course, all these other women started staring and giggling."

"The store had a whole wall of bras. I hurriedly picked one out, but of course mine was at the top. My mom had to get a pole to get it down. Of course, I thought *I saw a boy I knew* and ducked into the dressing room. My mom just stood in the middle of the floor, calling my name, holding this bra."

bra necessities

Seeing your upper body grow before your eyes can bring out some *mighty strong feelings*—and a whole slew of wonders and worries. Like, how do you know when you're officially ready for a bra? What if you don't want one? What if you wish you had more to fill it out? We know there are a lot of mysteries out there when it comes to bras. The good news is we're here to shed some light on this whole bra business. **So here are all of your burning bra questions.**

Q: "I want a bra, though honestly, I don't need it. I just want it! Everyone else has one. What should I do?"

A: A lot of girls don't want to be first or last for anything, and you may feel wearing a bra will help you fit in. **Check the options at the store and tell your mom you'd like to buy a bra.** You can even try a training bra, which is a first-timer's bra made with developing figures in mind. However, for those who don't need a bra and are happiest in cotton tees and undies, don't worry about doing the bra thing. You'll have plenty of time to wear one later.

Q: "I want a bra, so how do I tell my mom about it?"

A: The best approach? Be straightforward. Talk about it. If you want a bra so you can feel like part of the crowd, just say so. Maybe drop a hint, such as, *"Megan and Emma are* wearing bras now. **Maybe 9 should, too."** If talking it over with Mom seems truly impossible, consider writing her a note or approaching a grandma, aunt, or older sister. They've all been there. If you're totally stuck, talk to your doctor on your next visit. **She can help you sort things out** and possibly even talk to your mom for you. But give it time. This is a transition for both you and your mom.

Q: "My mom wants to buy me a bra, but I don't want one and don't think I need one. Can't I just wear an undershirt?"

A: **Has your mom seen some changes you haven't noticed?** While many girls wait anxiously for signs of puberty, others have different things on their minds. So take an honest look to see if your mom is right.

Are you bouncing around? Are your clothes fitting right? Look around school and you'll see that quite a few girls are going through changes, too, and you aren't alone. If you still want another opinion, ask a friend what she thinks. And then give bras a try.

Q: "Isn't it so embarrassing to buy a bra in public?"

A: **You have nothing to be embarrassed about.** If you run into girls from school, you can console yourself with the knowledge that they're there for the same exact reason. That said, some girls would rather not have a sales clerk **screaming for a price check** while half the drama club is in the next line. One way to go is to shop at places you know you won't run the risk of seeing anyone else. Says Pam, thirteen, **"Once 9 knew how to pick my right size, 9 would go someplace 9 don't ordinarily shop, knowing no one would see me running in and out of the dressing room with**

41

ten bras in my hand." If you truly can't deal, ask your mom to buy a few bras on her next run to the mall. Try them on, and have her return those that don't fit. Or figure out your sizing using our chart, and have a parent order by phone from catalogs or online.

Q: "How do I find a bra for my breasts, which are two different sizes? Nothing fits."

A: As we said before, **this is totally normal** and nothing to panic about. **Many girls and women have uneven breasts.** It's not unhealthy or freaky or even worrisome. Styles with cups made of stretch fabric provide a better fit. But to get a true fit, you may need a half size, something not a lot of bra makers have.

Q: "I want to stuff. Is it a good idea?"

A: Stuffing horror stories abound. It never seems to fail that the day you break out the box of Kleenex is **the day your crush falls on top of you** in a freak cafeteria accident and a winter cold's worth of tissues goes flying in front of the entire school. Make peace with the figure you have. If you really want to pump up the volume a bit, **look for a lightly lined bra style** that will provide a bit more shape.

just your *size*

Can you believe that up to eighty percent of girls wear the wrong size bra? **Getting a good fit is especially tough when you're a teen,** as your body is constantly changing. So as you seek your first bra, it's good to know what sizing is all about. To start, your bra size is made up of two parts. The number is your frame size (30, 32, 34, etc.); the letter is your cup size (A, B, C, etc.). **To figure out yours,** take a tape measure and measure snugly around your ribs, just under your bustline.

(It may help to have your mom, a sister, or friend assist you.) If the measurement is an odd number, add 5. If it's an even number, add 6 (for example, if you measure 26 around, you're a size 32). Total them up, and that's your frame size. Next,

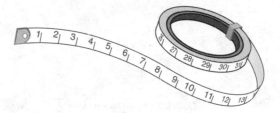

wrap the tape around your body again, this time measuring at the fullest part of your chest. Do this standing up straight, checking in a mirror that the tape is level. Subtract your original frame size from this measurement. Then check the chart below to figure out your cup size.

Measurement Difference	Cup Size
The same as your frame size	AA
Up to 1 inch larger than frame size	A
Up to 2 inches larger than frame size	B
Up to 3 inches larger than frame size	C
Up to 4 inches larger than frame size	D

bra flaws— fixed!

You're fairly sure you have the right band and cup size, but something just doesn't feel quite right.

★ **Problem:** My band is riding up in the back

Your bra band is too loose, your cups are too small, or both. Try going up a cup size or down a band size. And remember that a large bust needs a wider, closer fitting band than smaller busts to provide proper support.

★ **Problem:** I'm spilling out

Cups that are too small need to be larger (and vice versa), but changing the cup size can also change the band size. The C cup on a size 36 is the same size as a B cup on a 38. If you go down a band size, you'll go up a cup size. So try going a step up and down on the band and cup sizes until you get your perfect fit. And remember: **different bras are not created equal,** which means that even if you are **"technically"** a 34B, that doesn't mean all 34Bs are gonna work. We can't stress it enough, try on a number of styles and sizes.

★ **Problem:** My straps are sliding off my shoulders

The easiest thing to do is tighten them up using the adjustment on each shoulder strap. If you have very narrow shoulders or if they slope, look for sports bra-type cuts that have wider straps placed closer to your neck.

★ **Problem:** My straps are digging into my shoulders

Either your band is too loose or your cups are too small. If your bust is larger, you also might want to look for a bra that has wider straps.

taking care of
the skin you're in

4

You look in the mirror and there it is—staring right back at you. A pimple. A blemish. Why did this have to happen just when you want to look your best? (OK, so there's really never a good time, but still!) Why you?

No one knows for sure exactly what causes acne vulgaris, the technical name for a major breakout. But researchers do know it usually starts in adolescence and that heredity plays a big role. But don't think you're facing a bad skin day alone. Matter of fact, if you break out, you have lots of company—about eighty-five percent of the preteen and teen population has some kind of problem skin.

Luckily, most teens who break out only have a mild form called non-inflammatory acne, and get just a few blackheads or whiteheads every now and then. The less lucky suffer from the more severe form, called inflammatory acne. Inflammatory acne results in constant outbreaks, covering the face and sometimes also the neck, back, and chest. Unless you're careful, these pimples and cysts can cause deep pitting and permanent scarring.

all about acne

why pimples pop up

Acne attacks when glands that produce this oily stuff called *sebum* work overtime, **possibly due to hormonal changes during puberty.** One job of the sebum is to haul cells shed by the glands to the skin's surface.

But when too much sebum blocks the openings of the glands **(called ducts)**, cells and sebum build up, making a plug called a *comedo*. If the plug stays below the surface of the skin, it's really light and called a *whitehead*. If the plug gets bigger and pops out, the tip looks dark and is called a *blackhead*. This isn't dirt, and it won't wash away. The darkness is a buildup of *melanin*, the dark pigment in the skin. If this keeps up, a pimple forms.

Breakouts most often start around age eleven for girls and thirteen for boys. Scientists think hormones called androgens have something to do with acne. Among other things, androgens stimulate those darn sebum-producing glands. After puberty, boys produce ten times as many androgens as girls. No surprise, then, that more boys than girls get serious breakouts.

And even though there's a connection between the severity of breakouts and the amount of oil a person's skin produces, not all people with oily skin get zits—and some people with dry skin do!

47

sneak spot causers

☀ **stress.** If most of your breakouts are on the outer cheek, jaw, and chin, suspect stress. There is no medical treatment for stress spots. So eat right, get plenty of sleep and exercise (a proven stress reducer), and for goodness' sake, chill, girl!

☀ **cosmetics.** If you use any makeup product regularly and your cheek area is dotted with blackheads and whiteheads, you could be having a reaction, or the formulation just isn't right for your skin. Try hypoallergenic brands. Breakouts along your hairline? Switch your styling products, or forgo the goo altogether.

☀ **sweat.** If your only breakouts are small, inflammatory bumps on your forehead, chest, back, shoulders, and chin, you may have acne mechanica, which is caused by pressure, friction, and heat. Ditch the tight synthetic stuff for heavy workouts (they hold sweat next to your body), and switch to cooling cotton instead.

☀ **iodine.** There's a slim chance that your diet could be to blame for acne. If you eat tons and tons of iodine, you could be eating your way to a breakout. Highest sources of iodine include kelp, liver, asparagus, turkey, broccoli, onions, tortilla chips, chicken, beef, and iodized salt. Before giving up those foods, though, talk to your doctor. She'll be able to evaluate whether your diet is properly balanced.

avoiding—and attacking—acne

The occasional breakout can be headed off simply by **washing your face** once or twice a day. If that doesn't do the trick, it's time to try one of those **over-the-counter acne medicines** that you dab directly on the skin. Look for ones with benzoyl peroxide, sulfur, resorcinol, or salicylic acid—all of which really zap blemishes.

All of these drugs are **"peeling agents,"** which irritate and dry the skin. That might sound scary, but believe us, it helps loosen plugs and shed dead cells. The drugs can also make bacteria back off, which reduces the fatty acids that add to breakouts. **What won't work is picking at pimples.** This can damage your skin and its underlying tissues, and you could end up with major scars. So hands off!

Here's a battle plan to help you win the war against spots:

Treat breakouts the right way. Get zits only occasionally? Wash your face with a mild face wash in the A.M. and before hitting the sack. Follow with a moisturizer and zap whiteheads with a two-percent salicylic acid, on-the-spot product. Prone to major breakouts? You need an acne cleanser. Spot-treat pimples with a benzoyl peroxide product. If acne is persistent (aka, doesn't clear up after two weeks), see a dermatologist—a doctor who specializes in treating and curing acne.

Go easy on your skin. Sure, it's easy to get angry when blemishes are bustin' out all over the place. But an all-out assault on your skin is only gonna make the sitch worse. The biggest mistakes you'll make with your skin is squeezing or picking pimples and vigorously scrubbing your face in an effort to get rid of acne (or prevent it). Start a fresh mitts-off policy and stop popping—pronto.

Watch out for hair hazards.

Who knew that hair products can wreak havoc on your face? The scalp line and areas covered by hair can develop more clogging of follicles, leading to blackheads or whiteheads—especially if there are also products like gels, mousse, or styling lotions in your hair. So try pinning your bangs back with an assortment of headbands. Take a break from hair products, too, and see if that helps your skin. If you can't part from the gel, make sure to cleanse your face after your hair is styled. And wash strands before bed, so they don't ick up your face while you're sleeping.

Cleanse right after your workout.

When you work out, you gotta get rid of the

grease straight after a sweat sesh. Waiting will just allow the sweat, dirt, bacteria, and other inflammatory agents to work against your new clear skin regimen. Keep a box of wipes in your gym bag; they make it easy to stay on top of your routine, especially after hectic away games.

no more body bummers

Body breakouts bringing you down?

☀ To control all-over zits, wash your bed sheets every four days. Bacteria and dead skin accumulate (ew). Also, avoid hanging out in your workout clothes or damp swimsuit.

☀ In the shower, try an anti-acne body cleanser. Every other day, follow with a body exfoliator. For hard-to-reach spots, get a back scrub and massage brush.

Eat and drink your way to clear skin. Even though certain junk foods have a bad rep for causing acne, experts say there's no direct link. That said, having a healthy lifestyle may help control breakouts (and is generally a fab idea anyway). So power yourself up with super food antioxidants like pomegranate, goji berry, and green tea to banish blemish-challenged skin. Or choose the trick many celebs swear by: chugging lots of H_2O. Another healthy habit all girls gotta get into? Beauty sleep! Skin makes vital repairs when you wind down. Just another reason to get eight straight a night (at least!).

Clean up your act. Your face isn't the only thing that's in need of a regular wash-up routine. It's super-important to keep everything around it way clean, too. Get in the habit of changing pillowcases about once a week (think of all the grime that builds up!) Use a face-only towel to avoid putting grime back on your skin. Oh, and if you wear makeup, degunk brushes on a weekly basis, too. Use warm water and brush cleanser to keep 'em sparkling. Just like you!

getting help from a pro

You've tried all the products, been patient and then some, and your face is getting worse, not better. It could be time to see a dermatologist.

On your first visit, she'll evaluate your skin's condition and prescribe some treatments that are stronger than what you can buy off the drugstore shelf. These include topical (things you can put on your skin) and oral (things you take by mouth) antibiotics.

After you've used a medication for a month, you'll be back for a checkup and your dermatologist can switch treatments to something less harsh or more effective, depending on your needs. With any product, things might get worse before they get better, but hang in there.

your acne questions answered

Q: "I have these tiny bumps on my upper arms, legs, and on my butt. I don't think they are pimples. What are they and how can I get rid of them?"

Q: "My friend swears by a great benzoyl peroxide product. So I went out and got some, and nothing happened! What gives?"

A: What works for your friend might not work for you. You'll probably need to try a few formulations to see what clears your skin best. Test the products on the back of your hand first, to make sure you won't have an allergic reaction to it or it doesn't cause excessive redness, dryness, or peeling. If your hand looks normal after twelve hours, it's probably OK to use the stuff on your face. And remember, **pimples don't go away overnight**—be patient and hang in there. It doesn't last forever—it just feels that way. If it persists, you may want to consult a dermatologist.

A: You're right, they're not pimples. Although their raised, red appearance do make them dead ringers. Those bumps are probably something called keratosis pilaris, which is a buildup of dead skin. How to treat? Experts recommend a moisturizer that's at least two-to-six percent lactic acid. Make sure to use after bathing so that the skin can more readily absorb the lotion. Leave the loofahs off your skin: Harsher scrubs can only irritate the skin and cause more dryness. And no picking!

Q: "Chocolate and French fries don't make me break out, right?"

A: Correct. It's a myth that chocolate and junk food make acne worse. However, a good balanced diet is important to your body. And since your skin is the body's largest organ, it will benefit from lots of good-for-you food and from drinking at least eight glasses of water and three glasses of milk a day.

Q: "I have the world's greatest skin—until right before my period. What's up with that?"

A: Blame it on hormones. A lot of girls get zapped with one or two pimples two to seven days before their periods start. At the first sign of trouble, dab on a treatment product. Be careful of going hog-wild with medicated cleansers, toners, and astringent pads. Most of your face is probably still dry or normal, so don't turn the whole thing into a peeling, pimply mess—just hit the spot.

Q: "Can medicines make acne worse?"

A: Yes. Many medicines may do this. If you think the medicines you are taking have made your breakouts worse, you should speak to your doctor. Never, ever stop medication on your own, and never take someone else's medication. Your doctor will help.

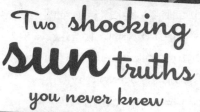

Two *shocking* sun truths

you never knew

1 **Exercising outdoors increases your risk of skin cancer.** Makes sense that girls who spend a lot of time outdoors get more dangerous sun exposure. But get this: High-intensity training may actually suppress your body's immune system, leaving it less able to fight off cell damage caused by UV rays. The double whammy? Sweating can make it easier for the skin to absorb harmful UV light because the sunscreen can wash off. Slather on plenty of sweat-resistant SPF 30+ and reapply often.

2 **Your eyes need protection, too.** Mom always told you never to look into the sun, and while her reasoning may have been off ("You'll burn your retinas!"), she was onto something. Keep the delicate skin around your eyes safe with big, wraparound shades that block sun from the sides (nothing cute about crow's feet at eighteen). Look for sunglasses that protect from UVA and UVB rays.

Q: "Can makeup cause breakouts?"

A: Makeup is usually fine as long as it's a hypoallergenic, water-based, or noncomedogenic product. The most common culprit is oil-based foundation—steer clear. And no matter what kind of makeup you wear, be sure to take it all off at night.

Q: "I heard the sun is good for your skin."

A: That color you got over spring break can actually lead to big problems. Your face probably isn't used to strong sun, and that glow you got is actually damage. And damaged skin tries to rebuild and repair itself by shedding dead skin cells. This can lead to dead skin debris clogging oil glands, which leads to breakouts. Yet another good reason to SPF-it to the max, don't you think?

sun truths—exposed!

startling stats

Sure, a tan can look great, but it comes at a price—serious damage to your skin. According to the American Academy of Dermatology, one blistering sunburn during childhood nearly doubles your lifetime risk of melanoma, the most aggressive form of skin cancer. Plus, more teens are being treated for sun-related skin damage than ever before. Even scarier: The rates of melanoma are rising among women fifteen to thirty-nine, according to the American Cancer Society. Think you're safe because you have dark skin? Think again: No one is safe from the sun's damaging rays. No one!

People with darker skin have a lower risk of skin cancer, but that doesn't mean they're in the clear. Truth is, skin cancer has been diagnosed in people of all races and descent.

test your *sun smarts!*

1 **What's the first thing you do when you hit the beach?**

A. Set up an umbrella in the sand, strap on a huge sun hat, and reapply the SPF 50.
B. Rub on whatever sunblock is buried in your bag, then hit the waves.
C. Break out the mags, strip down to your bikini, and plunk down on a towel for an afternoon in the sun.

2 **When are you most likely to go for a walk or run on a summer day?**

A. First thing in the morning or when you get home in the evening.
B. You prefer to go in the cooler morning hours, but sometimes you'll go out in the afternoon, if it's not too hot.
C. Midday. All of that fresh air and sunshine perks you right up!

3 **Do you wear sunscreen when it's cloudy out?**

A. Of course! Even on cloudy or hazy days, unseen ultraviolet sun rays can cause unexpected sunburn and skin damage.
B. Sometimes, though, you often forget.
C. Nope. What for?

4 **Finish this sentence. Sunglasses are for . . .**

A. . . . blocking out harmful UV radiation as well as UVA and UVB rays.
B. . . . preventing you from squinting.
C. . . . looking hot, of course!

5 **Have you ever used a tanning bed?**

A. No way! Hello, claustrophobia!
B. A few times, but you prefer the real deal to the fake-and-bake.
C. Yup. If it's raining out, you're there.

now, tally up your answers and see how smart you are about your skin.

Mostly A's:
sun smarty

No one needs to remind you to lather on the SPF this summer! You're super-smart about the sun and protecting your skin from harmful rays. Whether you've got a history of skin cancer in your family or you're just cautious about your health, you've got every reason to steer clear of the sun. But don't let your vigilance spoil your fun this summer: It's OK to get in a few minutes of rays here and there (and knowing you, you'll have the SPF in hand. Smart!).

Mostly B's:
partly cloudy

OK, you slip up once in a while and forget to protect your skin. So what, right? Actually, when it comes to the sun, inconsistency can be a big deal, as just one bad burn may double your risk of skin cancer. So do your best to maintain a regular skin care regimen: Wear SPF of at least 30 every day, see a dermatologist annually for a mole check, and don sunglasses with lenses that block out one hundred percent of UV radiation as well as both UVA and UVB rays. Got it? Good!

Mostly C's:
study up, sunshine!

Hello, sun goddess! You soak up the rays like it's your job and you probably have a great tan to prove it. But at what cost to your health? Even if you don't burn and lack telltale freckles or moles, no one's safe from sun damage. Plus, after years of constant sun exposure, your skin will eventually sag and spot. And who wants that? So cover up in the sun with SPF and a wide-brimmed hat. And if you must get some color, at least do it the sunless way with a spray tan.

protect
yourself

Even if you're just running across the street to say hey to your neighborhood crush, you're getting zapped by powerful rays. Same goes if it's cloudy out (a dreary day can still bring on unhealthful rays through the clouds). So protect yourself by slathering on the SPF (experts recommend SPF 30 or above) as part of your daily routine. And *reapply, reapply, reapply—especially after swimming* (the effects of sun exposure are cumulative—that means they add up). **The sun is strongest between ten A.M. and four P.M.,** so avoid direct sunlight at those times if possible. If you have to be in the great outdoors when the sun's at its peak, let us remind you: reapply, reapply, reapply.

In addition to being SPF savvy, you can actually dress for (sun-safe) success. **What to wear?** Here are some guidelines from the Skin Cancer Foundation: Hold the fabric up to the light. If you can see through it, UV rays can penetrate. **Darker fabric is better than light-colored fabric;** the thicker the cloth, the more protection it offers; and if the fabric stretches or gets wet, it loses much of its ability to protect you. For more guidelines, or to find out about products recommended by the SCF go to skincancer.org.

one more thing . . .

If you're really worried about a **mysterious mole,** if you've been overexposed, or you just sense that something's not right with your skin, **tell your parents,** then see a doctor right away. Chances are, it's nothing serious, but you really can't ignore anything shady when it comes to your skin.

what's the shelf life of my SPF?

Sunscreens come with expiration dates for a reason: The FDA requires sunscreens to be stable for at least three years, so check the date before you buy. Check the date, too, if you've pulled a bottle from way back in the closet with last year's beach gear. If it's expired, toss it. Don't risk using a sunscreen that may have decreased—or even zero—effectiveness.

SPF-15

but wait, don't i need to get some sun?

Not everything about sun exposure is bad news: Turns out, the vitamin D you receive from those rays may have a role in fighting off a bunch of bad things, from high blood pressure to cancer. But a new study says teens are lacking the levels needed to get the healthy benefits.

While the "sunshine vitamin" is best absorbed through the skin, there are other simple (and safer!) ways to get it. Drink plenty of milk, for instance (look for "vitamin D-fortified"). Eggs and fish—especially salmon and tuna—are great options, too. And don't rule out the outdoors entirely. Thirty minutes in the sun (yes, while wearing a high SPF!) will get you the D you need.

mouth matters

Obsessed with your mouth much? You're not alone. Whether you're worried about bad breath or constantly checking for food in your braces, you probably take plenty of peeks inside your piehole throughout the day. After all, your teeth—and mouth—are front and center in your world. Your smile (and your breath!) are some of the first things people notice when they meet you.

Needless to say, from dealing with braces to bad breath, there's a lot to think about (and a lot of action to take!) when it comes to you keeping your choppers clean. But no need to stress—here's all the info you need to keep your breath fresh, your braces blingin', and your mouth magnificent!

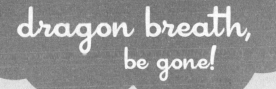

dragon breath, be gone!

It stinks having bad breath. But take comfort that a lot of us deal with this issue (also called *halitosis*). **Hundreds of species of bacteria live in our mouths,** feeding on food particles and saliva. They're actually doing this to keep our mouths clean. Thing is, as bacteria gobble up our leftovers, they create waste that smells *yucky.* The odor occurs because bacteria produce sulfur compounds. Other common causes of bad breath are hunger, dry mouth, and strong foods like garlic and onions.

The best way to freshen breath is to kill the bacteria. Always brush your teeth after you eat, rinse with antiseptic mouthwash, and floss daily. And, drink lots of water to wash away food particles.

And don't forget about your tongue, which is covered by tons of taste buds, called *papillae*. In between the papillae are grooves where food and bacteria collect, turning your tongue white and your breath icky (bleck). So when you brush your teeth, **also gently scrub your tongue with a dab of toothpaste.** Chewing sugarless gum after a meal is an easy quick fix, but if you still have problems, see your dentist to make sure you have healthy gums.

metal mania

You just found out you're about to get wired, or maybe you're **bracing yourself** (sorry, we couldn't resist) for the future possibility. You have tons of questions. **Do braces hurt?** How long do I have to wear them? Will I be forced to give up popcorn and candy? **Will I look like a geek?**

In addition to getting the scoop straight from the orthodontist's mouth, we asked our tin-toothed **GL** readers to give us the lowdown on their own experiences. After talking to more than one hundred and twenty girls, we can tell you this: Most girls say braces really **"aren't so bad"**—and that they're definitely worth grinning and bearing. As for your other biting questions, we spit out the answers for you right here.

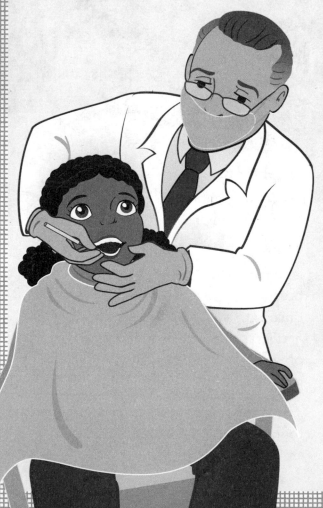

do you take good enough care of your teeth?

IF YOUR PEARLY WHITES HAVE TURNED TO GNARLY YELLOWS, MAYBE IT'S TIME TO START BRUSHING UP ON YOUR DENTAL HYGIENE PRACTICES.

1 It's friday, 10:30 P.M. you . . .

A. think, "Oh, well," and conk out on the couch.
B. suck water out of your toothbrush and barely touch your teeth.
C. brush for two whole minutes with the best kind of toothpaste you have.

2 After breakfast, you . . .

A. brush, brush, brush!!
B. forget about brushing! You are running way late!
C. squeeze a blob of toothpaste about the size of a pencil tip and brush for about twenty seconds.

3 To you, dental floss is . . .

A. a craft supply.
B. a bother.
C. your best friend.

4 Your breath usually smells like . . .

A. your little sister's tooty-frooty *Sesame Street* toothpaste.
B. mints.
C. old gym socks.

5 At the dentist, you usually have . . .

A. no cavities.
B. one or two cavities.
C. three or more cavities.

scoring **1** A. 1, B. 2, C. 3 **2** A. 3, B. 1, C. 2
3 A. 1, B. 2, C. 3 **4** A. 2, B. 3, C. 1 **5** A. 3, B. 2, C. 1

5-7 points
Better Brush Up
Wake up and smell the toothpaste. Introduce your mouth to a toothbrush and floss, like, fast!

8-11 points
Halfway Hygienic
You're on your way to toothy health, but your teeth could stand a little more attention. Brush at least twice per day and don't forget your tongue!

12-15 points
Totally Toothy
Way to go! You're your dentist's best bud. And no need to worry about stinky breath around your crush . . .

63

Q: "Why do I need braces?"

A: *Well, your teeth are crooked* and need straightening. You may have 1) buck teeth (your upper front teeth stick out farther than your lower ones), 2) an overbite (your upper front teeth cover your lower ones more than halfway), 3) an underbite (your lower front teeth overlap your upper front teeth when you bite down), 4) your teeth are overcrowded, or 5) there's too much space between your teeth.

Q: "How do I know if I need braces?"

A: *See an orthodontist* (or *"ortho,"* as girls say), a specialist whose job it is to prevent and treat such problems. During your visit, the doc will do an exam with **X rays.**

Q: "When should I go to an ortho?"

A: Many girls have their first visit when permanent front teeth come in, **about age seven.** The ortho can predict potential problems with your jaw and teeth. **The sooner you address the problem, the less time you'll have to wear braces.** The average age girls get braces is ten or eleven.

Q: "How long will I have them?"

A: Everyone's teeth are different. However, the average amount of time for wearing braces is **eighteen months to thirty months.**

Q: "Do they hurt?"

A: OK, we won't lie. **Your teeth will feel sore the first few days.** Orthos also recommend rinsing with warm salty water and sticking a bit of wax over any trouble spots where braces wreak havoc on the sensitive skin in your mouth (you'll get a free sample of wax). Almost all the girls say you'll hardly notice your braces after a week or so, except when you go for occasional tightenings.

Q: "Tightenings?"

A: Don't panic. Braces train your teeth to position themselves a certain way. Every so often, the ortho needs to tighten the brackets so they're still doing their job. It's pretty quick. You can also talk to your ortho about taking medicine for the pain.

Q: "Will my social life be over?"

A: Hardly, especially since so many other kids wear braces. Says Christina, twelve, **"After a while, you forget you have braces. They just become a part of who you are."** As for being teased, no worries. Only a few readers say they get teased, and as one girl put it, "Who cares? I'm going to have awesome straight teeth when they're off!"

FOR THE NEW "BRACEFACE"

"Check your mouth with your finger or tongue before leaving the orthodontist's office so you'll know if there is a wire sticking out. It'll save you the annoyance of having to return the next day."
—Heather

"Always brush or floss your teeth after a meal. I walked around with a blueberry stuck in my braces one day. How embarrassing!"
—Valerie

"Think about choosing the right color for your braces. I chose navy and yellow, which made me look like a bumblebee."
—Anonymous

"If your ortho tells you to wear rubber bands with your braces, do it. It'll make the time you have to wear braces much shorter."
—Pam

Q: "Do I have to get silver braces?"

A: No. In fact, one reader "got clear, so they aren't so obvious." One cool thing is the choice of colors for bands. **"Some people just pick metal,"** says Amy, eleven, **"but I pick a different color combo each time I go."** Other choices include yellow, orange, pink, gold, bright purple, green, anything!

Q: "Is there anything I won't be able to eat?"

A: There are definite no-no's. Steer clear of hard, sticky, or chewy foods since they may snap the wires or loosen the brackets. So buh-bye to caramel, taffy, peanut brittle, hard candy, etc. As for gum? **"I had gum one day, and the bracket fell right off,"** says Casey. Also, be careful with carrots, apples, and other crunchy fruits and veggies. And keep in mind, you break the rules and break your braces (brackets can get knocked loose, bands come off . . .), they're just gonna stay on longer.

Q: "What about food getting stuck in them?"

A: It happens. Scarlet, fourteen, says, **"Getting food stuck in your braces is the only really embarrassing thing, especially broccoli and tomatoes."** What can you do? Carry a toothbrush, and use it after every meal. Some readers ask good friends to clue them in when there are particles on the braces. A small pocket mirror doesn't hurt either.

Q: "What is head gear?"

A: Headgear, or a night brace, is a **metal wire that hooks to your braces, with a strap that circles your head.** It corrects a jaw that sticks out too much or not enough. The bad news is you'll look like Saturn. The good news is it's usually worn only at night.

Q: "How about a retainer?"

A: It's a single-wire appliance to be worn for a while after the braces come off, **just to be sure the newly straight teeth don't shift.** Some girls only have to wear one on the top teeth, but others have to wear one on bottom, too. **The best part is mastering the 360°,** a technical skill using your tongue to flip that baby around in your mouth. (Careful, though, they can actually break that way!)

Sore Subjects

Got sore spots on your tongue or inside your cheeks? If the sore has a white or gray base with a red border, you have a **canker sore.** Canker sores are caused by almost anything—braces, brushing too hard, biting the inside of your mouth. Though fairly harmless, they may be a sign of a poorly functioning immune system or vitamin deficiency if they last more than a week. To treat canker sores, rinse with an antimicrobial mouthwash to reduce irritation. Also, **avoid spicy and acidic foods,** and keep up good brushing and flossing habits to ward off bacteria.

tin pride

WHILE MANY GIRLS SAY THEY DON'T MIND WEARING BRACES BECAUSE OF THE FUTURE PAYOFF (STRAIGHT TEETH), A SURPRISING NUMBER OF GIRLS SAY THEY LIKE THE LOOK OF BRACES.

"They're like having an extra feature, giving me even more personality."
—Rachel

"I've had mine for two years, and I like them. I have even seen people wearing fake braces just to look cool!"
—Erin

"I think braces look really good on a lot of people. I always wanted them as a little kid."
—Jessica

"I think my braces make me look older. I like them."
—Anonymous

Thumb-Sucking Trouble

Addicted to sucking your thumb? You're not a bad person for finding comfort in the act, **but you are damaging your choppers.** The upper teeth will begin to protrude forward while the lowers draw inward. Look for other ways to soothe yourself—reading, taking long baths, or talking on the phone. You can also put icky-tasting polish on your nails or wear cotton gloves to bed. A therapist can help you beat this habit for good.

one more thing . . .

You want your teeth to stay healthy for a looong time, *so take care of 'em!* This means seeing your dentist twice a year (that's on top of your regular orthodontist appointments), brushing carefully after every meal, and flossing. That way, your pretty smile will last a lifetime!

more totally typical body changes

6

So, now that your brain's busting with all sorts of info, you probably think you've got your body covered from head to toe, right? Well, we hate to break it to you, but there's a boatload of other body issues you're bound to deal with now and into adulthood. Yep—as if your head's not already spinning from all of those changes in your body, more and more things will start shifting (and, in some cases, stinking).

So, to help you navigate this unpredictable road your body's on, here's a guide to getting past all sorts of weird and wacky stuff you may run into (if you haven't already!).

oh, the odors . . .

No one naturally smells fabulous. Why? Well, during puberty, your body pumps out heaps of hormones—the same ones that cause you to sprout up new hairs and breasts. These hormones send your apocrine glands, located under your arms and around your privates, into action. These glands regulate your body temperature, but they also produce a milky, oily kind of perspiration. The problem is, **bacteria thrive in this type of sweat,** and the result is a not-so-sweet smell simply known as body odor (aka B.O.). You can't really miss this telltale musky scent, which may remind you of a combo of onions and sweat. Ick.

But as bad as the stench of B.O. may be, the good news is that it's super easy to, well, wash away. Start with a daily shower, and lather up with an antibacterial deodorant soap. Then, dust your body with a light talcum powder to absorb moisture, and use a deodorant that's also an antiperspirant—it covers odors and dries up moisture.

Deodorant
24 Hour
Protection

And as you pick out your outfit, grab clean clothes that are **free of old sweat and bacteria** (the smell stays in fabrics until you wash 'em). Throughout the day, cut down on caffeine, which sends your apocrine glands into overdrive, and instead *drink plenty of water* to flush weird-smelling toxins from your system. Tried these steps and still smelly? See a dermatologist. It's not uncommon for some girls to need a stronger prescription deodorant to take care of the prob.

Help!

"My deodorant makes me itch like crazy! My mom said it might be the fragrance, so I tried the unscented kind but that didn't help. Could I be allergic to it?"

You may be. Most of the time, this kind of reaction is caused by a sensitivity to chemicals creating the scent in your stick. And even those labeled unscented may still feature some fragrances that'll bother sensitive skin. So avoid that annoying itch with a hypoallergenic and fragrance-free product.

"My BFF has body odor. Do I tell her? She'd be embarrassed if she heard it elsewhere."

Yikes. Sometimes the truth hurts, but when it's your friend, you have to be honest. If you had a big piece of spinach stuck to your front tooth, you'd want her to tell you, right? Buy some deodorant at the drugstore, and encourage her to try "this great new deodorant that doesn't leave shirt stains." **If she doesn't take the bait, it's time for a heart-to-heart. Let her know that, because you don't want people talking behind her back, you have to tell her something that might hurt her feelings. Then explain that she doesn't smell so fresh and might want to switch to a new deodorant.**

71

The Agony of Da Feet

So maybe you've banished B.O. **but still have a stinky sitch— with your feet.** Folks have been dealing with pungent piggies since shoes were invented. Why? Blame bacteria (yeah, again). The sweaty and damp conditions of your shoes help those microscopic organisms multiply, causing that not-so-swell odor to come creeping out of your shoes. And depending on the kind of bacteria found on your feet, some people's *tootsies* stink extra bad.

To minimize foot funk, always wear cotton socks and try alternating among different shoes each day, giving each pair time to dry out (cleaning them regularly helps as well). And when you're just hanging around at home, **go barefoot.** That includes skipping socks while you're sleeping. Bacteria are eliminated when your feet have a chance to breathe—and that way, others around you can breathe easy, too.

All of that bacteria and sweat that sends you to stink town can affect other parts of your body, too. Like your head—or more specifically, *your hair.* Overproductive glands can cause an oily scalp, which may turn your lovely locks into **greasy strands** and even dredge up the dreaded dandruff.

Yep, that's right: Dandruff is caused by excess oil, not dry skin, which is what most people blame for it. Here's what happens: All of us have a harmless little fungus living on our scalps. Sometimes, too much of this fungus can cause our scalps to shed skin cells too quickly. These cells are really sticky and form tiny globs of white flakes we know as dandruff. While it won't hurt you, dandruff can be embarrassing, especially when you're wearing a dark-colored shirt.

Luckily, it is easy to control with antidandruff shampoos. They keep that little fungus at bay, making your scalp less flaky. Look for dandruff shampoos that contain ingredients like **salicylic acid, zinc pyrithione, or selenium sulfide.** After diligently lathering up for a week, you should have a *flake-free head—and shoulders.* If the flakes come back, you should probably use a dandruff shampoo on a more regular basis.

Got Lice?

Oh, no! The school nurse just diagnosed you with head lice. You shower! You lather, rinse, and repeat! How could this happen? Don't fret—you're just another one of the **"chosen"** approximately nine million people each year infected by these tiny blood-sucking insects.

Help!

"My hair smells awful no matter how much I shampoo. Could it be from my pool's chlorine?"

If your hair smells like bleach, blame the pool. Chlorine wreaks havoc on hair. The cortex (inner layer) of your hair is protected by the cuticle (outer layer). Further, a natural oily substance from the scalp, called sebum, shields the strands. *Chlorine sucks sebum out of the hair,* **causing split ends and smelly strands. Wear a swim cap to keep water away from your tresses. Even better? Put conditioner on your hair underneath the cap. Also, use special swimmers' shampoo and conditioner as soon as you get out of the pool.**

So how were you lucky enough to get bugged out? Lice typically seem to favor straight hair and are transferred by **sharing hats, combs, brushes,** and even just simple head contact. They cling to the hair and lay eggs, called nits, *which are visible.* Once the lice attack, your scalp can itch and become crusty. Banish these critters with an over-the-counter medication containing permethrin. **You should also try to pick out the eggs with a special nit-removing comb.** Then get rid of the bugs forever by washing all your brushes, combs, clothes, and sheets in hot water. And we do mean all—those critters are persistent!

Losing It

Flakes and oil aren't the only thing that may be going on with your hair—some of you may be feeling a little lighter in the locks department. Shedding strands when you brush or as you wash your hair? It may freak you out to see that hair fall out, but it's important to realize that everyone loses hair—up to one hundred strands per day. When

you lose a hair, it's replaced by a new one growing in the same spot just below the surface of your scalp. Blondes may appear to lose more because they typically have more hair follicles than brunettes or redheads.

When you lose hair, check that they're breaking from the roots, not the shaft. If the hair loss is sudden and actually clogging up the drain, the usual problem is one called telogen effluvium. Huh? Basically, *your hair sheds prematurely,* but will regrow. It's like losing a baby tooth—the new tooth comes in eventually. Though rare, there are other causes for shedding, so if you're worried call around and find a derm who's comfortable treating hair loss.

the business on body hair

And while we're on the topic of hair, you may realize that you've got it popping up in all sorts of places besides your head. This is just another fun part of puberty, and it is, once again, totally normal.

If you're self-conscious about body hair, ask the folks if shaving your legs and underarms is OK. They might freak at first—not over your request but because it can be as stressful for some parents to deal with you going through puberty as it is for you. Give them a few days to mull it over rather than expecting an immediate nod.

As if all that new hair wasn't enough, some girls find it growing on places that, well, you'd rather it not grow—like on your breasts or above your lip. No need to run to the doc for this dilemma—it's totally normal. Around eleven or twelve,

certain hair follicles respond to hormones surging through the body, including your breasts and around your belly button. Some girls just develop more body hair than others.

There are options to get rid of unwanted hair such as waxing, shaving, or tweezing, but you should talk to a parent first.

Help!

"I'm the only one of my friends who doesn't shave, and it's embarrassing! I know my mom will say no if I ask. What should I do?"

Explain to Mom how embarrassed you've become. No mom wants her daughter to feel awkward and ashamed. Definitely avoid the "everyone is doing it" routine—moms hate that one! Tell her you understand it's a commitment, and that you know your hair will likely grow back thicker and darker, and that you're fully aware of the risk of nicks and cuts. If she knows you're down with the details, she might feel comfortable giving you the green light. Tell her you don't want to start shaving without her OK—but that you're ready.

❖

"I made a huge mistake a couple months ago. I tried shaving my arms, and now the hair keeps coming back all stubbly so I have to keep shaving them. Is there anything I can do to fix this disaster?"

Shaving doesn't make the hair come back any thicker or stubbier, but, it does make it come back, initially, shorter. And since shorter hair hasn't been worn down, it isn't long enough to bend. Until the hair gets "older," it will feel stubbly. By continuing to shave off the stubby hair, it is never given a chance to "grow up" into a long, worn-down, softer hair. So stop shaving those arms now. With some time, your prob is pretty much solved.

glasses, contacts, and other eye issues

Another area of your body evolving at warp speed? **Your eyes.** As you age, your eyes do, too, meaning many of you may have to get that first pair of glasses. Others might already be sportin' specs and are ready to make the switcheroo to contacts. (And, of course, there are more than a few of you who've been blessed with 20/20 vision and will never have to worry about this stuff. If that's you, skip this section, you lucky gal.) Whatever your eye issues are, we know you have questions. We have answers. Read on—with adequate lighting, of course.

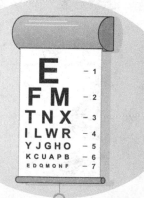

Need to Get Glasses?

How to tell if glasses are in your future? Well, obviously your best bet is to get a proper eye exam from a trained professional, especially if you're not having your eyes checked regularly at school. *If any of the symptoms below sound familiar,* you may want to ask Mom or Dad to make you an appointment with an eye doctor.

- ☀ **Trying to read the blackboard is like trying to read a fortune cookie message at the bottom of a pool from the high dive.**

- ☀ **The objects you see tend to be blurry, as if you were running by them at top speed.**

- ☀ **You're constantly being made fun of because of all the squinting you do.**

- ☀ **If you cover one of your eyes with your hand, you can actually see better.**

- ☀ **You keep mistaking your favorite fuzzy slippers for your dog.**

look spectacular!

☀ *oval face* Go for frames that are as wide or wider than the broadest part of your face. Cat's eye glasses are purr-fect for you.

❀

☀ *square face* Get an A in geometry by putting square faces with simple, rounder shapes.

❀

☀ *round face* It's hip for round faces to be square. Try boxy shapes for a fashionable edge.

❀

☀ *long face* Why the long face? Don't let your glasses make your mug anything less than cheerful. Look for extended corners and rimless bottoms that give your face a wider appearance.

In all seriousness, if reading this book is no prob, but everything's blurry when you try to look at something far away, you're probably nearsighted. If you are farsighted, it's the opposite. The words on this page may be *swimming* before your eyes, but you can easily make out the words on a poster across the room.

Glasses Do Not Equal Geek!
Stressing about your specs? **Think you're going to look like a geek?** Forget four-eyes and think fierce! If you pick up any fashion magazine you'll notice your favorite celebs have turned eyeglasses into fashion over the past couple of years. Looking smart today equals glamorous— and it's about time!

the big switch: glasses to contacts

There are many reasons girls opt to switch their specs for **contacts.** Maybe you want to show off your eyes. Or perhaps you don't want to deal with scratching, breaking, or misplacing your glasses. Whatever the reason, *it's a big step for you and takes a lot of responsibility.*

For some of you, the thought of sticking two lenses in your eye every day may **totally freak you out.** (Though once you get used to putting contacts in, you'll **never** know they're there.) Others may not want the task of properly cleaning, disinfecting, and storing contacts. But if you're ready to **tackle** all that, talk to your parents first. If they give you the thumbs up, have them take you to an optometrist.

eye yi yi
From seeing spots to styes, here's some info on other peeper probs.

"I see these shapes that look like what you see under a microscope, like bacteria or something. It's as if they're swimming in my eyes! What is that?"

The dark dots, lines, or particles you see are called **"floaters"**—aptly named because they seem to float in front of your eyes. They are actually shadows cast by the retina (that's the light-sensitive tissue lining in the back of your eye that helps you see). Floaters come and go when you move your eye, like when you blink. Although floaters can be a symptom of eye problems, like a rip in the retina, most cases don't threaten your vision. Most people in their teens and twenties notice spots at various times. If you're **nearsighted,** you may see spots even earlier. Most people just learn to ignore them. If they get worse or are bothering you like crazy, make an appointment with an optometrist.

79

⟳ **"I have this gross bump on my eyelid, and it's so painful. What is it?"**

Sounds like a sty—a red, painful lump caused by a bacterial infection at the root of your eyelash. It fills with puss and swells, though fortunately, sties usually disappear in a few days. You can relieve the pain by applying a warm, damp cloth to your eyelid for ten minutes, four times a day. To prevent further infections, keep the area clean and dry. Also, wash your hands frequently, and keep them away from your eyes. If the sty stays or affects your vision, see your doc. She might prescribe a topical antibiotic cream, or pierce the pesky lump to relieve pressure.

⟳ **"No matter how much I sleep, I have dark circles under my eyes. Why do I have them, and what can I do?"**

Dark circles can be a result of heredity, *allergies,* or sun exposure. They can also be caused by not drinking enough water, or nasal congestion. Don't lose any sleep over it, though— just a dab of concealer will hide those circles. **Choose a color that's a shade lighter** than your skin tone, and avoid white. For those with darker skin, choose yellow-based concealers, which counteract the blue in dark circles. Some research also suggests vitamin K helps fade 'em.

eating right
and getting fit

7

*I*t's no surprise that a lot of girls are constantly concerned with their bodies (if you weren't, we wouldn't have written this book, duh!). Given all the crazy changes that we've talked about, it's not suprising that many girls are confused about how much they should weigh, what they should eat, and how they ought to look.

We don't blame you for being so confused—there are a lot of conflicting body messages floating around out there. Here's the good news: Armed with up-to-date info, you can feel a lot more empowered inside and out. And just for you, we're dedicating this entire chapter to help you understand, take care of, and appreciate that awesome body of yours.

the skinny on fat

In today's **"thin-is-in"** world, fat can be seen as an evil thing. But listen to us **carefully: You need fat to live!** It's your body's main source of energy, and you must have it to thrive and exist as the energetic, active gal that you are. We all store fat in deposits around our tummies, thighs, and other places. When you need energy, that's what you automatically use! And it takes energy to do everything from running to texting. Not surprisingly, **some people store** **more fat than others**—usually because they take in more fuel than their bodies can use.

And what about the fat in food? Again, it's a necessary nutrient, just like protein, carbohydrates, vitamins, and minerals. Your body needs fat in foods to help you absorb vitamins A, D, E, and K—and, well, to make stuff taste yummy! (You just need to be careful about how much you consume, but more about that later.)

am i fat?

It's too bad everyone worries so much about weight. When we asked *GL* readers about body concerns, their most frequent questions were along the lines of, **"Am I fat?"** Our advice is to worry more about health than appearance. The best way to get an idea of your overall health? Calculate your Body Mass Index, a ratio of height to weight. Do this by dividing your weight (in pounds) by your height (in inches, squared). Multiply the total by 703 (or just Google **"BMI calculator"** to find a tool that lets you just plug in your figures online).

If you fall in the eighty-fifth to ninety-fifth percentile, you're at risk for childhood diabetes, heart disease, and certain cancers. Conversely, a lower BMI puts you at risk for other probs, like anemia.

But it's not as simple as that. For example, muscular, athletic girls can have a higher BMI, but be perfectly healthy. That's why the absolute best way to determine if you're at a healthy weight is to talk to your doctor. Some experts even warn that BMI is an **outdated** way to figure out if you're healthy. That's why being up-front with your doctor about your eating and exercise habits and talking about all your concerns is key to getting your most accurate evaluation.

10 insta-switches you CAN make today:

1. **talking on your cell? don't sit!** Walk around while catching up on gossip.

2. **put low-fat milk in your hot chocolate** instead of whole milk. A yummy treat, especially when it's chilly.

3. **give mom and dad a break** when you need to go somewhere. If you can get there safely on a bike or by walking, do it!

4. **put salsa or hummus** on chips instead of saturated fat-laden dip. Swapping baby carrots for chips makes it even healthier.

5. **hit the stairs instead** of the elevator or escalator. If the escalator is your only option, walk up instead of standing still (just be careful!).

6. **can't live without sugary cereal** in the morning? Go for it, but go halfsies with the more healthful high-fiber kind. You'll get the taste you crave and a punch of nutrition too.

7. **try d.i.y. yogurt.** Mix plain yogurt with the fruit of your choice. Add a little honey to make it sweeter.

8. **replace your morning OJ** with an orange. Real fruit is packed with much more fiber.

9. **dress up your salad** with peppers, mushrooms, nuts, dried fruit, chicken, pears . . . anything! So not boring and way better than plain old iceberg and dressing.

10. **clean your room!** Not only will you feel fabulously organized, but it burns about two hundred calories per hour.

the Unavoidable Weight Gain

At this time in your life, **it's totally normal (we repeat, normal!)** to put on the pounds. You're body's blooming, you're growing, and you're gaining muscle—and all lead to weight gain. Of course, there are genetic factors at play, too—when both parents are overweight, kids are eighty percent more likely to share that trait.

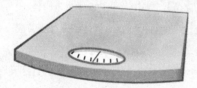

The only healthy way to lose weight is to eat more healthful foods and move around more while letting the pounds slooowly peel away. *Crash diets and crazy exercise programs just don't work.* Instead, it takes time to develop better-for-you habits and learn to (gasp!) enjoy exercising.

Learning to Love Your Curves.

No rock-solid abs? No worries! The truth is most of us will always have a little belly no matter what we do. Whether you're thin or overweight, everyone stores fat in different places. And where you store yours—your belly, thighs, breasts, or butt—is pretty much determined by genetics. Meanwhile, there are those blessed few females who have naturally *nonexistent* tummies. But before you get all jealous, know that they have fat stores elsewhere. So belly up to your natural body type, and learn to love it as is.

the thin truth

A small percentage of girls are naturally rail thin. **Sadly, these gals beat up on their bodies, too.** They worry that they're too bony, awkward, lanky, or boyish. They also field comments from people wondering how they stay so thin or falsely accusing them of having *eating disorders.* If you're naturally thin, you might fill out a little more after puberty, but then again, maybe not. If you're determined to bulk up, **certain exercises, like pushups, pull-ups, and squats,** can help give you muscle-y curves. Otherwise, you can't do much but learn to love your lankiness.

So when is being too skinny a problem? Anytime you're already thin, but are dieting or trying to control your weight anyway. If this is the case for someone you know, she could be suffering from an eating disorder (lots more on this subject in the next chapter).

Skinny vs. Fat: Who's Healthiest?

When we ask girls about their biggest body bummers, we mostly hear about weight. Heavier girls wish they had slim thighs like their thin friends. Skinny girls envy the curves of their voluptuous buds. While bodies come in all sorts of fabulous shapes and sizes, there is really only one ideal type for a body—healthy!

Many girls think looking slim **equals being healthy—**but don't let looks fool you! Sometimes skinny girls have non-active lifestyles, while some bigger girls are more active. How do you find out if your body is at its best, no matter what the scale says? **You know you're physically healthy when your heart rate hits two hundred beats per minute during rigorous exercise** (ask your gym teacher to test you).

And there are risks to being too thin or too fat. **Girls who are underweight don't develop strong bones.** From ages nine to fourteen, you develop the bone mass that stays with you the rest of your life! Undernourished girls miss out on necessary nutrients. Meanwhile, bigger girls get the nutrients they need to get through puberty and tend to have strong bones. But they could be setting themselves up for *diabetes and heart disease* later in life. The bottom line? Neither extreme is good for girls.

SIMPLE WAYS TO GET MOVIN'

* ☀ Walk your dog.

* ☀ Throw Frisbees, **fly kites, or buy sports equipment such as Velcro paddles and tennis balls. Now, get out there and play!**

* ☀ Do your chores. **Yard work, cleaning house, and washing cars are good exercise. See if your parents will throw you some dough to do more around the crib.**

* ☀ Watch TV. **Really. Just make sure you do jumping jacks during the commercial breaks.**

* ☀ Make outdoor plans with friends. **Instead of a pizza party, have a picnic by the playground.**

* ☀ Sing karaoke, **and boogie down.**

* ☀ Go puddle hopping. **Just be sure to hose off before stepping onto Mom's white carpet.**

* ☀ Baby-sit. **Take the little ones outside to play, and let them run you ragged.**

* ☀ Climb a tree—**you're never too old.**

excuse busters!

GOT A MILLION REASONS WHY YOU CAN'T WORK OUT? NOT ANYMORE.

"I'm sooo tired."

If you've got that sloggy, "I need a nap—stat" feelin', it's because, um, you aren't exercising. Yup, working out actually makes you energetic.

"Sweat? Ew! I would work out if it wasn't so gross."

Your body has to get rid of toxins, and sweating is a great way to do it. Plus, that glow is how you know you're actually working out and not just hangin' out. And, that's what a shower's for!

"I'm naturally skinny, so why should I exercise?"

Exercise is not about being skinny! It is about being strong, healthy, and respecting yourself.

"I don't have time."

Make time! If you're super-busy, split up your workout. Do ten minutes in the A.M., then another ten at night. Sneak in longer workouts on weekends, like hIking or an extra-tough bike ride—whatever it takes to get moving, do it!

"I'm a first-timer . . . and I don't know what to do!"

It can be overwhelming at first, but there's sooo much info out there (visit girlslife.com). And don't be afraid to ask for help, whether it's from your sporty BFF, your athletic brother, or your PE teacher.

come on, get healthy

Whatever your body type, there are some simple steps everyone can take to treat your body as the temple that it is. All you've gotta do is eat right, exercise, get plenty of sleep, and drink tons of water. Easy, right?

Well, not always. In this go-go-go world, we're all guilty of making some body-busting moves, like staying up way too late working on a history paper, selecting soda over H_2O, and fueling up on fast food. Once in a while, it's okay to fall off that healthy track. But if you make a habit of dissin' your bod, it'll smack ya right back with icky sicknesses, less energy and focus, and bad skin, just to name a few.

But we know you've got what it takes to treat your bod right. You may just need a little help along the way. And that's what we're here for! We've laid out a simple plan for you to follow that'll have you feeling—and looking!—fab.

Step 1 *eat right*

Nearly twenty percent of kids think they're overweight, so it's no wonder lots of girls want to shed pounds. But if you've tried dieting, you know it sucks. *Eating nothing but carrot sticks can make you obsess over food.* Then your body goes wacky, trying to make up for calories it's not getting. Want a saner (and safer) way to peel away the pounds? Here's our advice:

Start the day off with a healthy breakfast
Go ahead—have the breakfast of champions. You are more likely to eat less the rest of the day than if you were to eat a **wimpy morning meal** or just skip it all together. We suggest scrambled eggs, toast, and a banana.

Dine often

Skipping meals doesn't make you **skinny, Minnie.** When you miss out on meals, your body conserves energy and burns fewer calories. Plus, if you eat only one meal a day, it's impossible to get all the nutrients you need. Your best bet is to eat **three same-size meals** and two small snacks each day.

Power up on protein

Science supports the notion that smart protein choices can help you lose weight. Why? Eating good proteins, like chicken, salmon, or beans, **leaves you feeling fuller.** Just be sure to round it out with healthful carbs, like fruits, vegetables, and whole grains.

Downsize

Portion control is the ultimate answer to your best weight. Easier said than done when packaged foods and soft drinks come in bigger portions than ever before. It's common to get **thirty-two-ounce** sodas, which are loaded with hundreds of extra calories. One serving of meat should be about the size of your palm. A veggie serving is the size of your fist. Also, avoid eating straight from the bag—you almost always consume more that way.

Mix up your meal

Let's say you love brownies. But if you had brownies every day, you'd get sick of them, right? It's the same thing when you eat a meal. After the first couple of bites, your taste sensors become **duller** and you don't enjoy it as much as you did when you started. So, instead of eating your favorite part of dinner all at once, enjoy a little bite of everything on your plate. You'll feel more satisfied.

Snack smart

It's so tempting. You come home from school and those Cheetos are **beckoning from the cabinet.** Hard as it is, ungrab that bag! When you're starving, snacks loaded with refined carbs (chips, snack cakes, donuts) make you hungrier! How? They make your blood sugar levels **spike** and then drop dramatically. Then you're stark-raving hungry all over again.

๑ Drink up

You've heard it a thousand times, but it's true—**water is just plain good for you.** Six to eight glasses a day will keep your organs working properly and your skin clearer.

๑ Treat yourself

You promised yourself you'd never eat **Death-by-Chocolate** again. Uh-huh. We don't believe you. And, more important, you don't believe you either. But, unless you are truly bingeing, one particular food is not the prob. What's the problem then? It's the inability to eat the not-so-healthful foods in moderate amounts. If you say to yourself, **"I'll never have another cookie!",** you're much more likely to down a whole plateful. Ugh. Plus, why torture yourself? If you like cookies, go ahead and indulge. Just not every day.

Step 2 get moving

You should do some sort of aerobic exercise—that's anything that gets your heart **pumping**—for at least thirty minutes, five times a week. But where the heck should you start? Try a strength-training workout at least once a week, including thirty to forty-five minutes of sit-ups, push-ups, leg lifts, and other easy at-home exercises. Need some inspiration? **Try these must-do moves** (that'll work your legs, tummy, and give ya a cardio boost, too) three days a week:

✿ One-Legged Squat

Set up a chair so it's an arm's length in front of you. You'll use this for balance, if you need it. Lift your left leg slightly off the ground in front of you and keep your right leg planted. Reach your arms out in front of you as a counterbalance. Slowly squat down, until you feel like you're sitting in a chair. Stand up slowly. Repeat five times and then switch sides. Do three sets. If you're a beginner, start out with one set.

✿ Deck Squat

Start with your feet at hip-width apart, with hands by your side. Drop down to the ground in a squat position, with your butt tucked under. Roll onto your back. Don't roll onto your neck! Reach your hands out in front of you and roll up onto your feet. Stand up. Repeat five times, and do three sets.

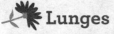 Lunges

Stand with your feet hip-width apart with your hands by your side. Take a big step forward with your left leg. Lower your right knee down, until it's almost touching the floor. Don't let your left knee extend over your left ankle. Your thigh should be parallel to the floor. Slowly stand back up and return to start. Repeat five times on each leg. Do three sets.

Push Back Push-up

Start standing, with your legs together, hands by your side.

Crouch down to the floor and get into push-up position. Do one push-up. Stand back up. Repeat five times and do three reps.

Five-Count Sit-ups

Hook your feet under a couch or have your workout partner hold them for you. Bend your knees and sit up with your hands behind your head. Slowly ease down to the ground. It should take you five full seconds to hit the floor. Return to a seated position in a five-count as well.

Step 3 sleep tight

With tons of tests and piles of papers, sleep is often the first thing you sacrifice during the school year. But when you don't get enough shut-eye, tests get harder, crankiness creeps in, and, well, everything falls apart. (On the flip side, get too much, and you'll still feel exhausted.) Girls your age require about nine hours a night, so try to get on a strict bedtime schedule (ten P.M. is ideal if you get up at seven A.M.) and avoid **buzz-causing drinks** like cola.

Step 4 *stress less*

Homework overload? Friendship drama? Whenever you're stressed, **a hormone called cortisol is released.** It causes the body to go into protection mode, meaning some girls get the urge to eat for comfort. The answer? Take a bath, exercise, read, shop—whatever. **Chill out**—and turn to Chapter 9 for other easy ways to relax!

one more thing . . .

Sure, it takes work to stay healthy. But just think of all of the benefits you're bringing your body: *You'll look great and feel better physically.* By making a few simple lifestyle changes, you'll have more energy, sleep more soundly, and be your fab strong self. These solutions work, and they're good for you—no matter what you weigh.

All about abs!

No need to fear a two-piece swimsuit—ever! We have fab ab moves to tone your tummy.

knees and elbows

Lie on your back, with hands clasped behind your head. Lift your knees, head, and shoulders off the floor. Crunch up until knees and elbows touch. Slowly lower yourself, without letting feet or shoulders touch the floor. Repeat twenty times without stopping.

bicycles

Lie on your back, with hands clasped behind your head and legs extended. Keep abs tight, and lift legs about an inch off the floor. Slowly bend your right knee, and twist your left elbow across until the two touch. Slowly straighten your right leg, and return the left side of your body down to the mat. Repeat on opposite side. Do thirty on each side.

scissors

Lie on your back with your hands planted on the floor underneath your butt. Lift your head and shoulders slightly off the floor while raising legs straight into the air (your body will be in an L-shape). Split your legs, with the right leg going closer to the floor and left leg toward your belly. Exhale and switch legs. Do twenty reps. Too easy? Do twenty more.

single leg stretch

Lie on your back with your arms and legs straight up in the air. Tighten abs, then lift your head and shoulders slightly off the floor. Grasp your right leg with both hands. Slowly lower your left leg until it almost touches the mat. Raise leg up. Repeat on the other side. Do fifteen on each side.

leg raises

Lie on your back with your hands on the floor under your butt. Leaving head and shoulders on the ground, raise both legs up until your body forms an L-shape. Slowly lower both legs down until feet are an inch above the floor. Slowly raise them back to start. Repeat fifteen to twenty times.

More likely to give yourself "ughs" than "oohs" and "ahhs" in front of a dressing room mirror? Well, welcome to the club. Shockingly, more than half of U.S. teen girls feel their bods are flawed, not fab. Body-bashing is an all-out epidemic that comes in every shape and size: "My breasts are too small." "Mine are too big." "I'm too short." "I'm too tall." All the pressure—peer, parental, media, and cultural—makes it hard to feel good in your own skin.

We know, we know: It's not always that easy to love your looks—especially on those days when your hair's a mess, you've got a big zit on your forehead (on class picture day, no less), and you've sweated through your sweater (again). So to help you regain that lovin' feeling, here's a look at your biggest body image issues, plus bunches of ways to stop worrying about your "flaws" and accept that you are gorgeous, just the way you are.

love your body

First things first: You must realize that there is absolutely no one ideal body type for a woman. Nope, not even a supermodel's shape can be considered the standard—their skinny bodies (which are at least twenty-five percent lower in weight than the average girl) represent less than five percent of the U.S. female population.

And even though there's constant chatter on TV shows and on magazine covers about obtaining a flawless figure, you can never expect to achieve that level of perfection. Nobody can.

You see, everyone has flaws. It's hard for us to realize this, of course, when we're constantly bombarded with images of beautiful, **seemingly perfect pop stars,** actresses, and models. There is an enormous amount of pressure in our culture to be super-skinny, leading to unrealistic expectations that wind up weighing rather heavily on your shoulders.

Or maybe it's not just the media that's got you going mad about your weight. Maybe it's a little voice inside your head telling you that you'll be a faster runner, or a little more popular, **or your crush will finally ask you out if you lose a few pounds.** And then that quest to drop a pound or two turns into an obsession.

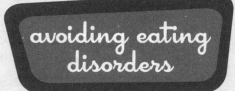

avoiding eating disorders

According to recent statistics, as many as ten million women are struggling with an eating disorder. Disordered eating is serious and becoming more prevalent in middle and high schools and even elementary schools. If you're feeling pressure to be thin or find that you are obsessing over food or exercise, please know that an eating disorder is not going to solve any of your problems. In fact, it's only going to make you feel worse. Not only will it take an extremely serious toll on your health, **but eating disorders can be deadly.** If you're weighed down by negative thoughts about your weight, then you need to talk to a doctor, counselor, or other health care professional. You can feel good about yourself, but it's up to you to take that step.

a quick guide to eating disorders

here's what you need to know about the most common eating disorders.

anorexia nervosa

Anorexia nervosa is a **potentially deadly** eating disorder. The sufferer intentionally starves herself and is unwilling **or unable** to keep a healthy weight for her size, height, body type, and activity level. She has an intense need for control and is scared of gaining weight even when extremely underweight.

compulsive overeating

The compulsive overeater, usually overweight, eats to excess even when not hungry, but doesn't purge. The overeater eats throughout the day, not just during binges. Health concerns, similar to people with clinical obesity, include diabetes.

bulimia nervosa

The bulimic often consumes large amounts of food in short periods of time—sometimes thousands of calories at one sitting—and then forces herself to purge by throwing up, exercising, or using laxatives. After bingeing and purging, a bulimic feels depressed or guilty. Like an anorexic, she is intensely fearful of being fat. In addition to causing major dental problems (from stomach acid), binge-and-purge cycles damage the digestive system and affect major internal organs, like the heart, which can cause death.

FOR SUPPORT AND INFO ABOUT EATING DISORDERS, CHECK OUT:

National Eating Disorders Association: nationaleatingdisorders.org

Something Fishy: something-fishy.org

The Renfrew Center: renfrew.org

yes, you can learn to love your looks

it might seem secretly fun and satisfying to realize that your legs are longer than the new girl on your volleyball team. But being dependent on another person to feel good about yourself never leaves you feeling self-assured for the long haul.

So perhaps your body isn't perfect. So what? You can still take the reins and make yours the best it can be. First step: Quit comparing yourself to others. Can't stand shopping because the clothes are never in your size? Whether everything's too big or too small, being on either end of the size spectrum is annoying. But just remember that in middle and high school, almost everyone's body is out of whack. Some girls are still growing, while others hit their peak in sixth grade.

Plus, there will always be someone who, in your mind, looks better—whether it's your favorite celeb or the girl who sits next to you in math. And yes,

It's like saying, **"I'm OK if you're not,"** which means someone else has to seem worse than you for you to feel better. Not cool! Believe that, even without comparisons, you are fabulous.

flip those flaws

Did you know that you have approximately two thousand body parts? That's a whole lot to love. So, it's reasonable to not be crazy about every single inch of your body. But as much as you'd like to trade in a couple of parts for new ones, truth is, you're stuck with what you've got. So show those heads, shoulders, knees, and toes some love!

And how to do just that? Think of a few positive traits. Maybe you have big feet, but they're probably what make you such a speedy swimmer. And those freckles on your face? A beautiful badge of your Irish

Is your bod a super-sized issue in your head?

Think outside the bod. Focus beyond your looks to find one thing that makes you feel like a superstar. A whiz on the computer? Use your skills to help your sis create an awesome website for her babysitting business. Love to bake? Wow the neighbors with killer cupcakes. And use your newfound confidence to walk tall, whatever your size. Remember, standing out is a good thing. How boring would the world be if everyone were the same?

heritage. You have great toned arms from softball? **Rock 'em in sleeveless tops.** You inherited beautiful brown eyes from your grandma on your dad's side? Show them off with golden eye shadow. You can't trade your body for your BFF's or anyone else's. So accept and love what you can't change. Soon, you'll find yourself more comfy in your skin. And if you think you look good, others are going to pick up on that vibe. Beautiful!

makes you feel more relaxed, happy, and confident because of all the endorphin-action that comes with a good sweat.

Sounds like a chore? Doesn't have to be. If you hate the gym, don't go. Don't like running? Skip it. Choose an activity you enjoy, whether it's biking, ballet, body surfing, hiking, or hula dancing! You'll be motivated to stick with it once you find your groove.

Be a Smart Cookie

Eat healthfully without being all obsessed with, "What do I weigh?" Making smart food choices may keep your weight in check, but it also plants a glow in your skin, adds shine to your hair, and majorly oomphs your energy level. No need to ditch the chocolate chips always and forever, but regularly substituting something like fruit or frozen yogurt is smart and

Shake Things Up

There's good reason to enjoy being active. Exercise not only makes you look your absolute best by toning muscles, it also

So Smooth

delicious. Even a slight change in your diet (like cutting back on your daily soda fix) has healthy benefits over time.

✿ Add Spice to Your Life

Boost confidence by taking on new (and fun!) activities. Joining drama club, volunteering at a pet shelter, taking dance lessons, or going out for volleyball can make you happier on the inside. And the more you're happy with who you are, the less things like your breast size matter.

body confidence:
still a ways to go?

WHAT PART OF YOUR BODY DO YOU LIKE BEST?

Curvy hips? Great calves? Strong arms? These are the kinds of responses we expected when we posted this question on girlslife.com. But no. It turns out girls love their faces, feet, and hands best. While we think it's great that you love your sweet mugs, it's obvious girls don't fully appreciate their shapes. Favorite features, starting with most popular, are:

1. eyes
2. nose
3. lips, smile
4. feet, toes
5. hair
6. hands, nails
7. dimples
8. belly buttons

Now don't you think it's time to start loving the rest of your body, too?

READY, SET, GO!

collect compliments

Do you shrug off all the nice things people say to you? Like, when your BFF says, **"You look awesome today!"** you say, *"Yeah, right!"* Well, shoo the nice words away no more. Of course it's not good to depend on compliments to feel good about yourself, but do yourself a favor and accept the kindness graciously. From this day forward, even if you don't feel like you're lookin' so groovy, when someone says something nice, respond with a simple, **"Thank you."** Later in the day, remember all the positive words you received. It works wonders to pump you up.

ban bad-bod chatter

Negative self-talk—whether it's aloud or in your head—is poison. Whenever you think something negative, like **"I'm fat!"** or *"I'm so ugly!"* stop that voice in its tracks. Instead, think something good about yourself. With practice, your self-critic will fade and you'll be **jazzed** about how you look—and feel!

Another great technique is to talk to the mirror. Every day, say upbeat things to your reflection:

"My hair looks great today," or, **"I'm a really good friend."** Talking to the mirror might seem a tad geeky at first—especially because you've been so busy bashing your looks rather than lovin' them up! But your self-esteem will rise with the sweet talk.

So take that energy you waste trashing your looks and put it into being a better person. Not only will it increase your self-esteem **and attract more friends,** but it will put your body image in perspective as just one part of Totally Irreplaceable You.

appreciate the package

Your self-worth shouldn't be about the wrapping. Lots of other things are more important. If you don't have it going on inside, looking good on the outside isn't going to cut it. Being friendly, outgoing, **upbeat,** kind, loyal, generous, and caring are qualities that make you attractive.

one more thing . . .

So how can you learn to love your sweet self just as you are? Looking for role models who love their looks is a good start. Instead of wishing you could look like a supermodel, focus on real girls with positive self-images. **And BTW, nobody cares that much about what you look like.** As much as you think everyone else is stuck on how you look, they aren't. Even your friends don't notice your left earlobe is longer than your right—unless you point it out, of course. So why worry?

what's your body confidence?

1 The idea of shopping for a new swimsuit next summer makes you want to:

A. book a trip to the beach. You love picking out the perfect swimsuits that show off your absolute best features.

B. get it over with. You don't mind the bathing suit pursuit, but the idea of being practically nude under bright lights is definitely no day at the beach.

C. land a killer internship in Alaska for the summer.

2 If you could only wear one outfit for two weeks straight, it would be:

A. a sundress and strappy sandals.

B. jeans and a tee.

C. X-large PJs.

3 When you change for gym class, you typically:

A. change in front of your locker, no worries.

B. face the wall and dress fairly quickly—this is not a floor show.

C. barricade yourself inside a bathroom stall with the door bolted shut.

4 Viewing yourself in the mirror sans clothes is:

A. a sight to behold!

B. tolerable to acceptable.

C. cruel and unusual punishment.

5 You would describe your bod as:

A. a work of art—Vermeer would have been inspired.

B. healthy. Hey, it does what it's supposed to.

C. the bane of your existence.

6 When you see a photo of yourself, your first thought is:

A. "I really need to get an agent."

B. "Some days are better than others, but not too shabby."

C. "From here on out, photographing me is officially prohibited."

7 When walking between two close desks in class, you:

A. plow right through without hesitation.

B. walk through sideways, inconspicuously, of course.

C. avoid the desk space altogether—even if it means walking a lap around the whole room.

Scoring

Mostly A's:
body proud

You go, girl! Seriously, you're one confident cat. You like what you see in the mirror and have no problem showing the world that you have nothing to feel embarrassed about. As long as you're careful to appreciate your fine self without body-boasting, you have no worries. Continue doing what you're doing—being exactly who you are!

Mostly B's:
body double

You seem to be walking the body confidence balance beam. You have moments when you wouldn't mind covering up in baggy sweats, but also times when you feel fabulous. But most days, you don't really even give it much thought. Why obsess over your body? All in all, you feel healthy and strong because you take care of yourself.

Mostly C's:
body bummed

You have a heavy issue here, and it's not necessarily your weight. It's one of two possibilities: 1) You are genuinely overweight and feeling terrible about yourself, or 2) You are perfectly healthy but can't see yourself for what you are. No matter which one is you, wake up, girl! There's no need to go through life feeling this way. Get to your doctor to have an honest talk. You'll get the real story on whether or not you have a weight problem. He or she can give you advice on being your healthiest—and refer you to a counselor who can help you deal with your negative thoughts.

tips on *boosting your body confidence*

✸ use your body.

Having body confidence means refusing to judge yourself based on what other people think. It is about appreciating the way your muscles and joints move when you kick that soccer ball down the field, dance in graceful circles, run as fast as you can, or sidestroke across the pool. Forget about what a scale or measuring tape tells you. Because when you think about it, your body is a pretty amazing thing—every ounce.

✸ raid your closet.

Get rid of all the clothes in your closet that don't fit and make you feel bad about yourself. You know—the sweater so tight that we know what bra you're wearing. Or the jeans that are so baggy, you could hide puppies in them. Trash them. By that, we mean give it to your cousin or bag it up for a charitable donation. Your unflattering clothes can make someone else feel great.

stop hiding.

The irony is that the more you try to hide yourself, the more you stick out. And everyone else is so worried about their own flaws and hang-ups, they're probably not noticing any of yours anyway. If you act confident, people will believe you are confident. And there's nothing more attractive than people who genuinely feel good about who they are!

face the mirror.

Yep, shed all your clothes and stand right in front of your mirror with the lights on and everything. (Just be sure to pull your shades down.) At first, you'll probably take note of all the things you don't like. But force yourself to figure out what you DO like. It might be your curvy hips, a beauty mark on your shoulder, freckles on your belly. Don't get dressed until you find at least three things you like about your body.

stop talking about it.

One reason girls flip out about their bodies is that they spend so much time chatting about how they hate their hips, who gained weight, and how many calories there are in breath mints. You can say to your friends, "You know what, I feel like we've worn out the topic of weight watching. Let's talk about something else." Do more active things together, like hiking or biking. If your friends can't stop focusing on body parts, fly solo and find something else to do that doesn't involve fat grams.

healthy mind,
healthy you

Sure, getting healthy includes being good to your body (think: exercising and eating plenty of nutritious foods). But that's only part of it. A healthy you is one who's happy, too. And this means loving yourself from the inside out.

Of course, it's not always easy to do that. You may hate the way your hair has a habit of *frizzing out* on the days when you really, really need to look good. Or that no matter how hard you study, your BFF always gets a better grade than you. But beating yourself up for things you can't control won't help—it'll only make things harder (and you'll only feel worse).

So that's why we're here: to remind you that the best thing you can do is to just be yourself (and love it!).

happy, happy, joy, joy!

Contrary to what some people think, happiness is a choice. Sure, **life's gonna steer your bike tires into a muddy puddle from time to time.** But happy people choose to feel positive despite the bad things that happen. Let's see how you're looking at life as a whole, zoom in on the things that might be keeping your finger off the joy button, and clue you in on amazing ways to amp up your days.

Tune In to Your 'Tude

Your first move toward being happier is to figure out your take on life in general. If you see your Big Gulp as half-empty instead of half-full, you're not alone. Lots of girls use negativity as a way to protect themselves from disappointment—often without even realizing it.

break outta the blues

ARE ANY OF THESE MOOD-MASHERS ROADBLOCKING YOUR HAPPINESS?

chicken little

If you're afraid of feeling "too happy," it could be because you believe happiness is temporary. You're scared you won't be able to handle a crisis if it happens, so you're always on edge.

BREAK THE HABIT. It all has to do with self-confidence. You do have what it takes to handle any problem life sends your way. Remind yourself of the tons of times you've triumphed over trouble.

the perfectionist

You feel you have to "earn" a good time. It's a sunny Saturday, and your BFF calls to invite you on a hike. You've got a Spanish test Monday, though, and think you don't "deserve" a break until you've learned all your vocab backward and forward.

BREAK THE HABIT. Chill out by realizing happiness is a part of life to be accepted, not earned. Learn to treat yourself well, and for goodness' sake, cut yourself a break! You'll be even more successful if you let yourself have a little down time.

gotta-have-it girl

You're convinced you'd be the happiest girl in the world if your crush asked you out. Or if only your family won the lottery and could move to Maui.

BREAK THE HABIT. Any single element will not make your life perfect. Real happiness draws from many satisfying sources, like fab friends, a good family vibe, and liking yourself as you are. When you're busy being bummed about what you're lacking, you can't actively enjoy what you do have.

cellar dweller

You keep your mood on low by replaying a yucky mistake in your mind (say, missing that basket and losing the state finals) over and over.

BREAK THE HABIT. Everybody flubs up, so accept that you're human. No matter how bad the boo-boo seems now, you can—and should—move on. Talk to your parents, an older sibling, or favorite teacher. They can offer perspective and remind you that you're capable of great things ('cause you are!).

113

seriously sad

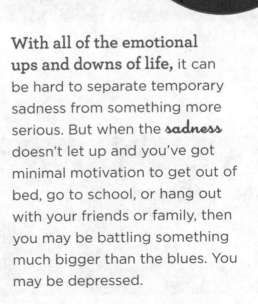

Say you failed a bio test, twisted your ankle in gym, and got dumped by your BF—all in one day. **Your mood's gonna stink** (of course!). But you know what? It's OK to be bummed when bad things happen, provided you don't get stuck in Glumville.

Remember, if you expect only rotten stuff to happen, you'll end up with a lot more bad days than you have to. You'll totally overlook truly great opportunities, **all because you're getting bogged down in the negative.** The key is to look at life in a balanced way.

When you're feeling gloomy, say to yourself, **"OK, I feel really gross about what's going on. So what can I focus on that's gone really well for me lately?"** Think about the props your coach gave you yesterday at track. Call a friend. The icky stuff is only a small part of your life.

With all of the emotional ups and downs of life, it can be hard to separate temporary sadness from something more serious. But when the *sadness* doesn't let up and you've got minimal motivation to get out of bed, go to school, or hang out with your friends or family, then you may be battling something much bigger than the blues. You may be depressed.

It's estimated that one hundred and twenty-one million people worldwide struggle with depression, a figure that includes up to one in five teenage girls. A mental illness that can be marked by feelings of helplessness, hopelessness, and despair, **depression** tends to hit teens hardest between ages fourteen and seventeen.

And although experts have yet to pinpoint depression's roots among teens, most say it usually has to do with a combo of genetics (you're at a higher risk if a family member has the disorder); **hormonal changes;** and increased pressure to look good and fit in with classes, sports, and friends.

Kind of like a bad mood that won't go away, depression can be downright debilitating. But you don't have to be in a constant state of sadness or sleepiness to be diagnosed as depressed. The condition can make you **extremely angry,** causing you to lash out at loved ones, get into fights with friends, and do other reckless and careless things.

depressed or just down?

You can't know for absolute certain if you have depression until you get a **diagnosis from a doctor.** But real depression is about more than just feeling sad, crummy, or dreary. Real depression affects your whole body—**especially how you feel, think, and act.** Depressed people hit low points a lot more than people who are just bummed out. Depressed people have bad feelings a lot of the time. What kind of bad feelings? Girls who have depression overwhelmingly feel sad, angry, guilt-ridden, anxious, hopeless, lonely, empty, worthless, or simply numb. **These feelings are intense**—and last for most of the day. Girls who have depression commonly have bad days every day for at least two weeks or more.

How you feel is strongly connected to how you think.

If your feelings are mixed up because of depression, then your thoughts will be, too. Girls who are depressed have trouble remembering, concentrating, or making decisions. If you're feeling depressed, your thoughts will be mostly **negative, exaggerated, or just plain untrue.** You might think and believe nobody loves you, everything is your fault, that you're not a good person and don't deserve to be happy, or even that you'd be better off dead.

As a result of all the inner turmoil, **things that used to be fun aren't fun any more** to a depressed person. Also watch for changes in appetite, excessive crying, shutting down, avoiding friends and family, getting in trouble at school, and **sleeping a lot** or not being able to sleep at all. Even doing a simple thing like getting up in the morning can be incredibly difficult for a depressed person.

getting help

If you think you could be depressed, confide in a trusted adult before things go too far. A parent, a school counselor, a relative, a close friend of the family, or a doctor—**go to anyone you feel like you can be honest with.** Keep reminding yourself that depression is nothing to be ashamed or embarrassed about, and don't let depression trick you into thinking that you can fix things on your own. You'll feel better a whole lot faster once you get help. Depression only gets **worse** when you don't do anything about it. Even if the depression is severe and has been going on for a long time, treatment for depression works.

a cry for help

Depression can be so painful that sometimes dying seems the only way out. The rate of teen suicide and suicide attempts among ten- to fourteen-year-old girls are on the rise.

So if you suspect someone you know may be suicidal, look out for these major warning signs:

Complaining of being a bad person or feeling rotten inside.

○

Girls at risk say things like, "Nothing matters," "It's no use," and "I want to tell you this, in case something happens to me."

○

Giving away her favorite things or throwing away belongings.

○

Becoming suddenly cheerful after a period of depression.

○

Hallucinations or bizarre thoughts.

○

Change in personality, eating habits, or sleeping patterns.

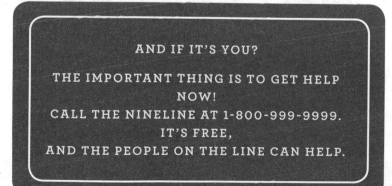

AND IF IT'S YOU?

THE IMPORTANT THING IS TO GET HELP
NOW!
CALL THE NINELINE AT 1-800-999-9999.
IT'S FREE,
AND THE PEOPLE ON THE LINE CAN HELP.

stress less

hide, experts say you should *buddy up* so that you're not stressin' solo. So call a friend to talk. Or even better? Laugh! Instead of a pity party of one, host a giggly get-together.

Even if you've got the whole happiness thing under control, chances are you still get super-stressed from time to time. (If you aren't? Well, what planet are you living on?!) In fact, a recent study by the Associated Press/MTV found that nearly half of teen girls report feeling frequent stress. The good news is that there are some simple steps, like these seven, to stop stress from ruling your world.

find a friend

On those days when you're so overwhelmed you just want to burrow under the blankets and

work it off

Another way to sap stress? Sweat! Of course exercise is good for your bod. **But a workout can work wonders on your mental health, too.** Vigorous movement, like dancing or sports, lowers tension and increases energy. Not too eager about exercise? All it takes is a quick walk to banish bad feelings.

eat right

Of course, eating healthy doesn't just do your body good—*it can also keep you calm.* Specifically, foods rich in folic acid and vitamin B (like salmon, brown rice, turkey, chickpeas, and bananas) have a soothing effect on the body, minimizing stress.

unplug and unwind

Think you'll just die if you don't text or update your online status every five minutes? **Think again.** Sometimes the best thing is to unplug, and you'll come back refreshed.

sleep more

The less you sleep, the more you'll stress. That should be a wake-up call to those who don't get their nine every night. **Try getting up at the same time every day,** even weekends. It may feel like a chore to climb out of bed at seven A.M. on a Saturday, but you'll be better off—and less burdened—because of it.

take care of number one

Always dashing to meet the demands of your parents, teachers, coaches, and friends? Being a people-pleaser is great, **but put your needs at the top of your priority list.** That means asking for help before the pressure causes you to lose your steam—and your sanity.

119

slow down

Swim team, school, soccer practice, Spanish lessons—sound familiar? If your stacked schedule's stressing you out, it's probably time to scale back. If you're feeling **overwhelmed,** the best thing to do is to try to slow down and take a break. Then, focus on your talents and strengths, whatever they are. What do you love to do, and what do you do best? By concentrating on the things you really dig, you'll be too happy to even think about stress.

How much stress is too much?

A little bit of stress is normal, but sometimes it can get outta control. If you find that it is interfering in your relationships, your activities, or your life, it's time to seek some advice from a trusted adult.

Warning signs to look out for include:

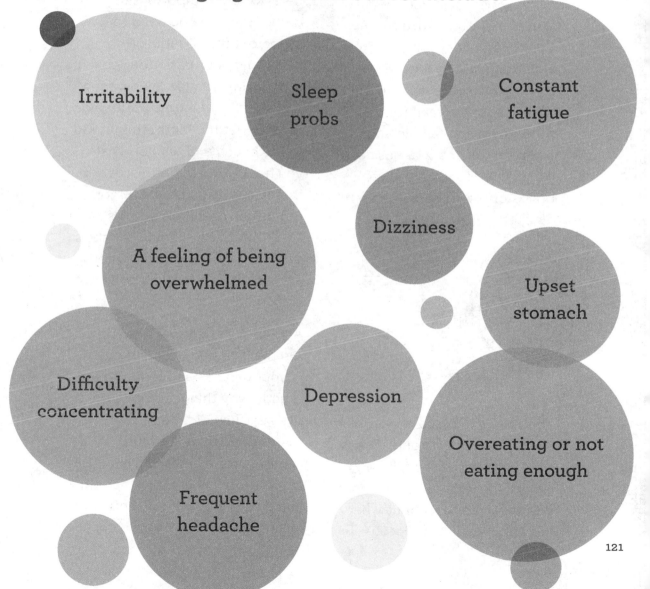

Irritability

Sleep probs

Constant fatigue

A feeling of being overwhelmed

Dizziness

Upset stomach

Difficulty concentrating

Depression

Overeating or not eating enough

Frequent headache

when things go *wrong*

So what to do when things go horribly wrong in your world? Well, for starters, take a deep breath, and tell yourself, **"I'm smart and strong enough to handle this—no sweat!"** Then don't doubt yourself for a second. Having faith in your ability to take care of business clears your head so you can brainstorm a solution.

Then you must face the problem. Don't go all ostrich and stick your head in the sand, hoping everything will magically disappear. Be real about what has happened, **and resolve to take action.** That said, don't strain your brain worrying about silly stuff that won't amount to anything. So you turned up at the Spring Fling in the same dress as that cheerleader Cara. **Who cares?**

It's also super-important to gather the info you need to scope out the situation. Rumor has it that your basketball coach is benching you for the next few games? **Before you freak,** you need to get the facts straight. Go to the coach and tell her what you heard. You might discover that it was just a bogus rumor. But if the coach tells you it's true? Talk to her about why she's sidelining you, and get pointers as to what you need to do to get back on the court.

And while it's natural to want to run the scenario over and over in your mind, trying to figure out exactly why things went down the way they did, **don't torture yourself!** Rotten stuff just happens sometimes. Say your BF Jason drops you for another girl. Sure, it's gonna bum you out, but talking about it with a bud can

really help. Know that you can't worry about it 24/7. It's crucial to keep the rest of your life **chugging** along strong. Stay positive by focusing on your favorite activities—hanging with your girls, reading mags, relaxing in a yummy vanilla-scented bubble bath.

Finally, sometimes, the only way to deal with a difficult situation is to make peace with it. With certain things in life, you can't affect the outcome. If your parents tell you that your fam's moving three thousand miles away, **then that's what's gonna happen.** Rather than losing it, get excited about the future. Just think about all the new friends you're gonna make and all the new things you can see and do! It sounds corny but, sometimes, what looks like the end of the world actually turns out to be the best thing that could have happened to you.

decisions, decisions

Another thing that's bound to throw you for a loop? **These ginormous decisions that have the power to change your life.** You know what we're talking about—like when you had to decide whether to take that trip to Hawaii with your family or go to band camp with your crew. You've always dreamed about seeing the Big Island, but you're also set on *snagging first-chair clarinet.* What's a girl to do? Well, no one makes the right choice every time, but with practice you can amp up your good decision-making skills.

dress rehearsal

You should give your decision-making chops a spin around the block on days you don't have something HUGE at stake. This is where the small stuff comes in. Should you drop your holiday cash on that awesome-but-pricey dress for the Valentine dance? Or should you put it toward your snowboard fund (you're so close)? Entirely up to you. But get into the habit of weighing options rather than making snap decisions.

the brain workout

Here's a little science lesson: Your brain is still developing, and your thinking skills are *flourishing.* When used, those cerebral connections strengthen. Yep, making consistently ace decisions is an acquired skill. **So by exercising your decision-making muscle, you boost your brain power.** Each time you wisely choose to, say, study bio instead of mindlessly texting your BFF, you're that much closer to setting your internal dials to **smart-choice** automatic pilot.

friendly fire

Like many girls, you might find yourself pressured by friends to do **seriously messed-up stuff,** like smoking, drinking alcohol, shoplifting, or cutting class. According to recent studies, the pull to maintain social connections can be ultra-influential and may motivate you to slip up in the decision-making department. Teens who have the most self-confidence are less likely to fall for the *"everybody's doing it"* hype.

There's no magic answer, but steer clear of the pressure cooker by going with your gut. If something feels wrong, it probably is. **Don't be caught off-guard —**if you're going to a party where beer may be on tap, think of how you will handle it ("No thanks, my parents would ground me 'til I'm gray"). Better yet, choose to skip the party and hang out with friends who don't booze it up.

a leap of faith

Maybe you have a big decision. The gymnastics championship you've practiced for all season . . . . or a trip to Vegas your mom won for being a top seller at work? Public school next year or private? **This is weighty stuff—**not like picking between a red cardigan or gray hoodie when getting dressed in the A.M.

Simplify the *overwhelming-ness* of it by writing a list of pros and cons, and jot your feelings in a journal. Go for a walk, or meditate. Consider how your choices will affect you, and keep your personal values at heart. **Read up, surf the web, and get sincere in-your-best-interests advice from a trusted someone.** Also, think about alternative solutions.

get over it

Good people make bad choices—**it's human.** Why dwell? Mistakes are lifelong lessons, so move on. If you took the wrong fork in the road, it's rarely too late to toss it into reverse. You joined a clique you thought was cool only to find out those girls are icky? *It's OK to change your mind!* No need to flatly announce you're no longer a member, but slowly disappear from their superficial world. You can make a conscious choice to rethink your original decision. (Which is why you should always save the receipt when you spring for a pricey dress. . . .)

one more thing . . .

Life will always be unpredictable. Don't bother wishing your brains out that nothing bad will ever happen to you—instead, know that you can take control of most sticky situations. Are you calm? For sure. Have the facts? Indeed. Clear on what's happening? Yep. Now, put your problem-solving plan into action. Then keep rockin' and rollin' at it until you feel better about what felt so bad—and yourself. You are so up to the challenge!

Index

The advice girls are looking for about practically everything!

From breakouts to periods, and everything in between, this guide delivers the body basics to help you look and feel fabulous!

Max out on your best moments with advice on how to handle first day jitters, fights with friends, and more!

You can't avoid ALL drama! This guide will help you deal with guys, friends, family, and more!

From classes to cuties to curfews—and everything else— getting exactly what you want is way easier than you think.

◼SCHOLASTIC

www.scholastic.com/girlslife

GLF10A